A PARENT'S GUIDE
TO
TEEN ADDICTION

Also by Laurence M. Westreich, MD

Helping the Addict You Love

A PARENT'S GUIDE TO TEEN ADDICTION

Professional Advice on Signs,
Symptoms, What to Say,
and How to Help

LAURENCE M. WESTREICH, MD

Skyhorse Publishing

Dedicated to Lisa, my wife.

CONTENTS

SECTION II:
SPECIFIC SUBSTANCES AND PROBLEMS

SECTION III:

THE BEST POSSIBLE TREATMENT

INTRODUCTION

If you're reading this, you must be worried about your teenager's use of drugs or alcohol. Fortunately, you can do more than worry: You have the power to wage guerrilla warfare against the substance habit that's invading your teenager's life. Like guerrilla fighters, you can use unconventional tactics to defeat this enemy—substance abuse or addiction—which is larger and more powerful than your family. *A Parent's Guide to Teen Addiction* shows you how.

This book focuses on practical information about everyday realities and techniques for helping your teenager. Rather than lecture on what constitutes addition, or how much substance use represents a problem, I'll show you how to identify the unmistakable signs of drug and alcohol use, and pinpoint the problems with your teenager's habit. Even when addiction is not involved, nonaddictive use or the simple misuse of a substance can still pose a problem. The *"Tough Talk"* dialogs throughout this book show examples of concrete, effective tools to get your message across to your teenager. You'll learn exactly what to say and the specific actions to take so they can resume a healthy, substance-free lifestyle.

Though I am an addiction expert and the father of two teenagers, I know of no cure for teen addiction. I do, however, have the expertise that comes from twenty years of evaluating, treating, and being there for teenagers who use substances. Based on my experience, the facts and strategies in this book represent the most solid information on teen substance use, the latest insights from medical literature, and the most beneficial treatment plans for substance dependence. Perhaps most importantly, I share what I've learned from families who set out to help their substance-using teenager win their war against abuse and addiction.

LOVE IS A BATTLEFIELD

Obviously, it's impossible to win this war if you don't know who the enemy is. Always remember that substance use—NOT your teenager—is your adversary. You might sometimes forget this if, like so many substance-using teenagers, your child has been taking advantage of you. Knowing that you want to see only the best in her, she counts on her trusting Mom and Dad to turn a blind eye to her drinking, drugging, or addiction. Knowing that she can get away with a lot of bad behavior, she might even manipulate her bighearted parents into helping her get drugs or alcohol. However, you're doing your teenager more harm than good by burying your head in the sand. To help her escape the control that substances have over her, you'll have to stop being a softy, and start being her firm, hands-on guide along the healthy and life-affirming path away from drugs, alcohol, addiction, and even death.

If you want to help your teenager beat drugs and alcohol, you'll have to work together with her as a family and use methods that may seem strange. The guerrilla techniques I offer sometimes contradict the received wisdom in the field of psychology. For instance, you might have to act decisively long *before* your teenager hits bottom. You might be forced to invade her privacy. It may also be necessary to temporarily abandon other priorities, such as her education, athletic ambitions, social relationships, and appearance, all in the service of fighting her substance dependence.

Like a guerrilla fighter, you'll have to react quickly and decisively to changes in the behavior of the enemy: substance use or addiction. Your retreat must be strategic, designed to advance your mission and energize your family to fight another day in the war for your teenager's health, well-being, and freedom from substances. You might, for instance, temporarily back off from your insistence that she go through the treatment that you and her clinician are pushing for. It may also be necessary, for the time being, to accept a setback in this battle in order to stay engaged with your teenager. Although alienating and perhaps causing your teenager to rebel against you might be inevitable during this process, at times you may need to act, or not, in order to preserve your relationship. Doing so lays the groundwork for an eventual victory over her substance use or addiction—when you get her into treatment and into a life free from her cravings.

THE BATTLE BEGINS

Helping families get their addicted loved ones into treatment was the subject of my first book, *Helping the Addict You Love: The New Effective Program for Getting the Addict into Treatment* (Fireside/Simon & Schuster, 2007). I found that each time I discussed the book with a new audience, the same questions would crop up: "Is it OK to snoop around in our 16-year-old daughter's room?" "What can we do to help our 14-year-old who drinks too much?" "Can the law help us get our 17-year-old son into treatment for his heroin addiction?" "Should we allow our high school senior and her friends to drink in our home?" This book will help you answer these and similar questions for yourself—and to act on your answers.

Section I, "What You Need to Know about Teenagers, Drugs, and Substance Use," lays out the facts of teen addiction and explains how to recognize a problem with your teenager. Section II, "Specific Substances and Problems," details what you need to know about the substances—alcohol, cocaine, marijuana, etc.—that teenagers commonly use. Due to their similarities to substance addiction, a separate chapter describes eating disorders as well as sex and gambling addictions. Additionally, the last chapter in Section II discusses dual diagnoses, in which mental illness and addiction intersect. Section III, "The Best Possible Treatment," provides information on exactly what to do about your teenager's substance use: How to find good one-on-one addiction therapy; how to encourage your teenager to enter different sorts of outpatient programs and inpatient facilities; how to line up aftercare treatment and get her to stick with it.

Throughout the book, I've transcribed a series of *"Tough Talk"* dialogs to show how other parents, teachers, and coaches have spoken with substance-using teenagers in some typical situations. Parents whom I've counseled have asked me the same questions you're probably asking yourself: "What should I do if my daughter denies everything? ... Lies to me? ... Blames the drugs or liquor on a friend?" Each dialog is an example of a positive, constructive conversation that you can have with your teenager. When a dialog strikes a chord in you, use it! Of course, you'll want to tailor it to fit your specific situation.

Use the book as you need to. If your teenager is in crisis and you urgently need to know what to do, turn right to chapter 10, "How to Find Good Treatment and Get Your Teenager to It." Not sure what's up with your teenager? Turn to the "Warning Bells" chart in chapter 2, "Recognizing a Problem," for help identifying the substances she's using.

Or maybe you want the big picture in order to put your teenager's problem in context: Start reading at the beginning of the book and you'll gain a firm foundation to support your efforts. You might already have a pretty clear picture of your teenager's condition and determined that it's not yet dire. Before things get worse—and to prevent that from happening—get to know more about the particular drugs she's using by turning to whichever Section II chapter deals with her substance of choice.

Like most parents, you love your child unconditionally: There's nothing she could do that would make you stop loving her. If she crashed your car, you would rush to the emergency room to make sure she wasn't hurt. If she were arrested, you would race to the police station to bail her out. Your love for your teenager is not a reward for her good behavior or high grades or athletic achievements.

We love our children unconditionally—what angers and sickens us is the grip that substances can have on them.

Your success in helping your teenager into recovery can be the beginning of a new and better relationship with her. Although I remind parents that they ultimately can't control their teenager, I assure them that they can often exert much more influence than they think. Time and time again I have seen parents cajole, manipulate, and even force their substance-using teenagers into treatment—for which they ultimately thank their parents. Do not give up. You are fighting the good fight!

SECTION I:

WHAT YOU NEED TO KNOW ABOUT TEENAGERS, DRUGS, AND SUBSTANCE USE

Chapter 1

THE FACTS ABOUT TEENAGERS AND SUBSTANCE USE

> When I was a boy of 14, my father was so ignorant I could hardly stand to have the old man around. But when I got to be 21, I was astonished at how much the old man had learned in seven years.
>
> —Mark Twain

It's natural for teenagers to test social limits on their way to becoming adults. As they start breaking away from their parents and defining themselves as individuals, they often become fascinated with drugs, alcohol, sex, and other temptations that are potentially harmful. I counsel teenagers who venture into this territory.

Experimentation with intoxicating substances can quickly lead to misuse and addiction. So, what's addiction? Like many substance use and addiction specialists, I define addiction as *compulsive behavior that a teenager keeps repeating despite negative consequences to his health, relationships, or performance at work or school.* When that happens, he can't easily stop what he's doing—even if he knows it's a bad idea.

For practical reasons, I deliberately define substance misuse and addiction in broad terms. Here's why: If your teenager's hurting himself with a substance, you probably don't care whether or not he meets research criteria for substance misuse or addiction, or if his suffering qualifies him for insurance benefits. You just want to get help. In fact, when I work with teenagers and their families I generally don't focus on diagnosis: it's enough that their son is causing himself some harm—or potential harm—with a substance.

OTHER DEFINITIONS OF ADDICTION

Addiction has been defined in many ways to reflect various perspectives. You'll find kernels of truth in definitions such as these:

From www.drugabuse.gov/publications/drugfacts/treatment-approaches-drug-addiction: "Drug addiction is a chronic disease characterized by compulsive, or uncontrollable, drug seeking and use despite harmful consequences and changes in the brain, which can be long lasting."

From the American Academy of Pain Medicine, the American Pain Society, and the American Society of Addiction Medicine: "Drug addiction is a primary, chronic, neurobiologic disease, with genetic, psychosocial, and environmental factors influencing its development and manifestations ... characterized by behaviors that include one or more of the following: impaired control over drug use, compulsive use, continued use despite harm, and craving."

This book concentrates on drugs and alcohol, but compulsive behavior around sex and food is a lot like misuse of or addiction to substances, and teenagers sometimes become ensnared in unhealthy eating or sexual behavior patterns. Chapter 8, "Addictions to Food, Sex, and Gambling" confronts such problems.

WHAT'S THE PROBLEM?

I use the terms "substance use," "addiction," and "dependence" somewhat interchangeably because I just don't think the differences among them are that relevant to your substance-using teenager. It's more productive to focus on specific problems that are the outcome of substance use, rather than on categories created for health insurance companies and research studies. By keeping this in mind, you'll avoid useless arguments about whether your child is an addict or is misusing substances, allowing you to move toward healing the damage to a person you care about.

The best thing to do when you know your teenager is experimenting with drugs or alcohol is to start talking about it. Initiate your conversations from a neutral perspective and focus on real-life problems instead of labels.

Tough Talk Dialog: "Dad, I'm Fine."

Hank: *So, how are you feeling this morning?*
Laura: *Fine, Dad. I'm fine.*
Hank: *I doubt it. After the way you looked last night, you must be hungover.*
Laura: *Are you mad?*
Hank: *I'm more worried, really. Even though you're a senior I want to know if there's anything I need to be really worried about—did you put yourself in danger last night?*
Laura: *Nope, I don't think so....*
Hank: *What happened?*
Laura: *Promise you won't be mad?*
Hank: *Can't promise that, but I can try. It's really important that you and I understand each other about this.*
Laura: *Well, Janie's mother wasn't home, so we all drank beers at her house. I think I maybe had five or six.*
Hank: *How did you get home?*
Laura: *Ellen's sister came and dropped us all off—she hadn't been drinking, Dad, so don't worry.*
Hank: *Well, OK. Were there any boys at the house?*
Laura: *No. What does that matter?*
Hank: *I worry that you could put yourself in danger—that a guy could take advantage of you when you're drunk.*

Laura: *Dad!*
Hank: *It happens, you know. (Hugs Laura.)*

In this conversation, Laura's father walks the tightrope that most, if not all, parents walk. While trying not to condone his daughter's behavior, he must acknowledge that substances can be used in a variety of ways, some terrifyingly dangerous and some relatively safe. He never agrees with Laura's choice to get drunk, but he does tacitly acknowledge that she has set clear limits about driving while intoxicated and putting herself in a vulnerable position with men. Although other dangers certainly exist—alcohol poisoning and the risk of addiction not least among them—Hank agrees with Laura's focus on the two potential dangers that seem to him most relevant to her situation. As a high school senior who will be going to college next year, she should be treated differently than if she were an eighth grader who came home drunk.

WHAT'S MY TEENAGER USING? HOW ADDICTIVE IS IT?

A yearly survey, done since 1975, of drug and alcohol use by high school and college students called "Monitoring the Future" shows that as of 2015 teenagers have started using more of certain addictive substances, while their use of others has plateaued. Among the 44,900 high school students surveyed at 382 secondary schools, it was clear that both usage patterns and attitudes toward drugs and alcohol are evolving.

At www.monitoringthefuture.org you can see which substances tenth graders used the most in 2016. Naturally, the percentages are higher when twelfth graders were asked the same questions, but you can see that the top three substances used by high school students are alcohol (43.4 percent of all students), marijuana/hashish (29.7 percent), and cigarettes (17.5 percent). Far fewer use substances that aren't on the chart, such as methamphetamine (0.7 percent), anabolic steroids (1.3 percent), Rohypnol® (1.0 percent), and heroin (0.6 percent). The *perceived risk* of marijuana use, as reported by high school students, has declined steeply since the mid-2000s.

Regardless of statistics, all you really care about is *your* teenager and what he might be drinking or using. Parents often ask me, "How addictive is the drug that my teenager's using?" The answer is complicated, but once again, it's specific to your teenager: Different substances affect people differently. You may know this from your own experience or from what you've observed in others. Some people take a Vicodin® from the dentist and dislike the "drugged" feeling, while others love it and try to repeat the experience for the rest of their lives. Some kids "specialize" in alcohol, while others rarely drink, but can't seem to live without cocaine. The chemical differences between substances affect how addictive they are, along with the physical and emotional makeup of the individual user.

One way to judge the addictive qualities of various substances is to look at how many people who *started* using a particular drug two years ago would be considered *addicted* last year. According to the Substance Abuse and Mental Health Services Administration, heroin, crack, and yes, marijuana, are the substances most likely to cause addiction in kids over the age of twelve.

THE SCOPE OF SUBSTANCE USE: FROM EXPERIMENTATION TO ADDICTION

As parents, most of us see experimentation with alcohol and drugs as a not particularly worrisome rite of passage. I believe that many, if not most, teenagers who experiment with drugs and alcohol don't become addicted. Nevertheless, even on its own, experimentation can still be dangerous. Where does the line between casual use and misuse lie? Parents often ask me, "Is she experimenting or is she addicted?" There's no hard and fast answer to that question, partly because the point at which experimentation breaks down into addiction isn't well-defined. Plus, there's a large group of "recreational users" who are hurting themselves with substances, but only a little bit. Further muddying the waters is the typical definition of experimentation as *any use that doesn't turn into a problem later.*

When does experimentation become misuse, and misuse, become addiction? As both an addiction psychiatrist and parent of teenagers, I often help other parents understand the various ways that their kids use substances—but I always focus on the actual dangers and avoid irrelevant discussions about diagnoses. Terms like "alcoholic" or "addict" mean so many things to different people that I almost never use them. Why bother? I usually tell parents something like, "It's clear that Sarah has a problem with cocaine—she's lost so much weight, and the coach has disqualified her from playing tennis."

No one likes to be pigeonholed, especially with a label that carries the stigma that "addict" does. It's much easier, and more useful, to own up to a concrete problem related to using a particular substance. It's also more productive to focus on the specific problems that arise from her substance use, rather than on artificial categories created for the convenience of health insurance companies and research studies.

Remember, *substance use* is simply the ingestion of any illicit substance. For teenagers, this includes alcohol and cigarettes. The simple fact of substance use isn't the only issue: what's important are the negative consequences of that use, such as the risk of addiction and arrest. In the case of *substance misuse,* the teenager experiences some negative consequences of using, short of addiction. For instance, if she drinks alcohol and vomits, she has misused the substance, but won't necessarily have any ongoing problems. However, she may move deeper into substance use and make more severe mistakes, such as consistently driving while intoxicated, missing school and work, or struggling with relationship issues.

In the most extreme cases of substance use, the teenager becomes dependent on or addicted to drugs or alcohol. Dependence might see her steadily using more and more of a substance than she wants to, because she's built up a tolerance and needs a bigger and bigger dose to get the same effect. An addicted teenager is unable to control or cut down her use. She spends most of her time searching for her substance of choice, ignoring important obligations in order to use, and going through physical withdrawal when she can't get the substance. However, your teenager may be dependent on a substance even if she doesn't undergo physical withdrawal or build up a tolerance.

REBELLION AND ADDICTION

Some teenagers may argue that addiction is just a social construct: One person's addiction is another's "partying" and you have no right to judge their behavior. He thinks that if drinking alcohol or using drugs doesn't cause problems for a kid, it's just fun, not addiction. You may have to teach your child that when it happens, addiction isn't just a matter of fun or bad behavior. Not that these aren't part of using addictive substances, but for many teenagers, by the time they realize they're not simply having fun, acting badly, or challenging you, they may be stuck with an addiction.

Using drugs or alcohol is frequently a way for children to rebel against their parents. Teenagers often defy their parents as a necessary part of transitioning away from childhood toward adulthood. This defiance often shows up in certain music, or styles of dress, and overall appearance that parents don't like. Drugs and alcohol often play a part in a teenager's quest to be an adult, as ways to separate himself from and, yes, frighten his parents. Every parent who has heard his teenager vomiting in the bathroom after overindulging in alcohol can attest to mixed emotions: fear for his child's well-being, anger at his teenager's bad judgment, and some satisfaction in the unpleasant, but non-life-threatening consequences his drunken teenager is experiencing.

It's important to remember that a teenager's addiction isn't only defiance of his parents and their norms. Even if he starts drinking or using as an act of rebellion, it can easily spin way out of control into addiction. In the words of one addiction specialist, for the addict, a substance has "hijacked the brain." Your teenager may have voluntarily let the hijackers in, but the bad guys are now in control.

Just as it's pointless to debate the definitions of substance misuse and addiction, it's not particularly worthwhile to dig up the reasons underlying your teenager's use. Alcohol or drug use that may have been a goof at the beginning has taken hold of your teenager's life, perhaps predictably from your point of view, but out of the blue for your teenager. If he's a problem drinker or user—or even a full-blown addict—first express your concern for him in genuine, caring terms. Criticizing him isn't going to help.

Tough Talk Dialog: "Marijuana is Natural!"

Karen: *Adam, Dad and I are so worried about your marijuana smoking.*

Adam: *I don't get it—why? I'm not hurting anybody. It's natural. It actually helps me study.*

Karen: *Well, we're worried about how you've changed over the past several months. The pot certainly hasn't helped you avoid failing your math class. Also, you're putting yourself in danger by buying it and having it on you—you could be arrested at anytime—you know that!*

Adam: *That's just not fair. Pot is so much safer than alcohol.*

Karen: *Maybe, but it's hurting you right now and you could get arrested for it. Whatever the broader issues may be, we're worried about you, right now.*

Notice that Adam's mother doesn't get sidetracked by his attempt to deflect the conversation into philosophical issues like marijuana's natural qualities. She also stays focused on her concrete worries for her son, and sidesteps his defiance about the unfairness of the marijuana laws. That's not the point right now and there's no need for Karen to argue about it with her son.

THERE'S NO SUCH THING AS A TYPICAL TEENAGE ADDICT

One misconception about drug and alcohol use is that rich kids with lots of unsupervised time on their hands are big users. In plenty of cases this is true. Ready access to cash certainly makes it easier to get ahold of addictive substances, but money doesn't make a teenager use them. Another stereotype is that street kids are heavy alcohol and drug users. Indeed, they sometimes are, but addiction doesn't discriminate; rather, it permeates all levels of our society.

Of course, if your teenager's addicted, all the truisms and statistics in the world don't matter. Just remember that your child, not you, is responsible for her behavior. This doesn't absolve you of all accountability for her addiction, but most of the responsibility lies with her. She's the one who needs to face the music and stop using. I always confront teenagers with this: if you blame others for your behavior, all is lost because you refuse to be accountable to yourself. Even acknowledging that parents make mistakes—we all do—your child shouldn't be allowed to shift blame. It's bad for everyone involved, especially your drug- or alcohol-using teenager.

WHERE TEENAGERS LEARN ABOUT DRUGS AND ALCOHOL

Teenagers learn about addictive substances from their friends, movies, and the media in general. Of course, more knowledge about drugs and alcohol doesn't necessarily lead to more use. Greater awareness of the damage they can cause often keeps teenagers from experimenting. In any case, there's little you can do to prevent your teenager from finding out about drugs and alcohol—you can't sequester him in the house forever. However, you can make sure that he's getting real information about the consequences of substance misuse, and help if he needs it.

The Internet is an uncontrollable source of information and misinformation about drugs and alcohol. Your teenager can easily find blogs and websites filled with dangerous misinformation if he wants to. Not only can he learn about addictive substances online, he can buy them there too. Anybody with an Internet connection and a credit card can order prescription drugs from illicit pharmacies, many of which are based overseas. Among the addictive drugs available online are opioids like Vicodin®, stimulants like Adderall®, and benzodiazepines like Xanax®. Watch your credit card bills and incoming mail, and turn the web to your advantage. Sites like those listed in Appendix B: Readers' Resources can give you and your teenager hard facts, guidance, support, and access to treatment information.

For the most part, though, teenagers get drugs from a more prosaic source: each other. Whether trying out different drugs at a party, rifling through the parents' medicine cabinet at a friend's house, or "lending" Ritalin® to help their best friend study, teenagers most often get drugs from other teenagers, either in exchange for money or as a gift.

Parents often encourage their teenagers to get involved in athletics and other extracurricular activities as a way to stay away from bad influences. Keep in mind though, by no means will this guarantee a substance-free life. In fact, the same social relationships that these activities foster can become relationships that promote drug and alcohol use. Even beyond potential challenges—like a football coach's unspoken encouragement of steroid use—your child might encounter groups of kids who use together as a way of bonding and experimenting in a less scary manner. I don't mean to discourage affirming and productive extracurricular activities, only to point out that participation doesn't necessarily protect teenagers from drugs or alcohol.

It's extremely difficult to prevent your teenager from hanging out with his friends, but you can keep your eyes open to who his friends are, where he goes, what he does, and whose parents are around (or not). Also, keep your ears open to slang words that you might not understand—familiarity with drug slang (see Appendix A: Glossary of Selected Drug Terminology and Slang) might indicate that your teenager is involved with drugs. If your teenager is drinking or using drugs with his friends, you might have to ban those friends, but be aware that this sometimes backfires. One thing that *is* completely within your control are the contents of your own medicine cabinet. Forewarned is forearmed.

POINTS TO REMEMBER

- Addiction is compulsive behavior that has negative consequences.

- Focus on how using drugs and alcohol actually hurts your teenager.
- Drugs and alcohol "hijack the brain," so don't waste energy blaming your own parenting skills.
- Don't just criticize your drinking or using teenager. Give him the benefit of your knowledge and life experience.

Chapter 2

RECOGNIZING A PROBLEM

Drugs are a waste of time. They destroy your memory and your self-respect and everything that goes along with self-esteem.

—Kurt Cobain (1967–1994),
lead singer and guitarist, Nirvana

As a parent, you're the one who should define when drug or alcohol use is a problem for your teenager, and how much of a problem it is. This is your right and obligation. Setting benchmarks for substance use and misuse is important not only for your sanity, but for mutual clarity as you guide your child in the right direction. When you have an unambiguous definition of the problem, it is easier to recognize. That said, it's also wise to watch out for certain concrete signs of substance misuse and addiction. The earlier you recognize misuse or addiction, the earlier you can get your teenager the treatment he needs—and the sooner he'll get into recovery.

DEFINING THE PROBLEM
The definition of addiction that I use—*compulsive use of a substance that harms a person's health, relationships, or school and work performance*—is broad, and it excludes the many kids who merely

experiment. Families define substance problems differently and set different rules around drug and alcohol use. I've worked with families who are so strict that they completely forbid any use of alcohol by their teenager, including at family meals, where a curious seventeen-year-old is allowed only grape juice while the adults drink wine. On the other hand, I worked with one family who tolerated their daughter's cocaine addiction because it allowed her to remain thin and keep her position on the gymnastics team. Between the polar opposite definitions of substance misuse—on the one hand, disallowing any use of potentially addictive substances, and on the other, acceptance of almost any use—lies the vast middle ground where most of us live.

You must decide where your family stands on your teenager's use of drugs and alcohol, and stick with your position. When I counsel families of substance-using teens, I ask parents to make the rules of the house and the repercussions of breaking those rules crystal clear to everyone. I can give input about what other families do and recommend techniques for keeping addiction at bay, but it's the parents who must make the rules and remain in control.

Regardless of the boundaries we set for acceptable exploration versus unacceptable misuse, we all know that experimentation with drugs and alcohol can sometimes develop into problematic use or addiction. Typically, using substances hurts teenagers in matters of physical and mental health, relationships, schoolwork, finances, and the law. Trouble that crops up in these areas is sometimes a red flag for teenage addiction. Keeping an eye out for any of these can help you recognize a problem.

HEALTH

Drugs and alcohol can harm your teenager's physical health in both obvious and not-so-obvious ways. The obvious ways are intoxication or withdrawal—a heroin overdose can kill by depressing the respiratory system and cocaine can cause heart attacks. The more subtle physical harm is what you'll see first, giving you the chance to intervene early on. Recognizing these effects can help you identify the cause and extent of your teen's problem. I label these as "early" and "late" effects of use to demonstrate that they will occur whether or not your teenager is physically addicted to the substance. All of these effects are warning signs about your teenager's behavior.

Physical Health Effects of Some Commonly Used Addictive Substances

Substance	Early Effects	Late Effects
Alcohol	Alcohol on breath Intoxication Vomiting	Slowed breathing Tremors Hallucinations Seizure
Barbiturates (Fiorinal®, Fioricet®)	Sedation	Overdose-level sedation Seizure on withdrawal
Cocaine/Crack	Agitation Tremor Bloody nose Burned lips and fingers	Chest pains Profound fatigue
Inhalants (Dust-Off, Nitrous, Kerosene)	Giddiness Disorientation	Paralysis Impaired memory
Marijuana	Lethargy Impaired judgment Increased appetite	Impaired motivation Hallucinations
Opioids (Heroin, Vicodin®, OxyContin®)	Lethargy Nasal pain	Slowed breathing Injection site infections
Sedatives (Xanax®, Valium® Klonopin®)	Lethargy	Agitation Seizure on withdrawal
Methamphetamine (Ice, Crystal Meth)	Agitation Irritability Grandiosity	Insomnia Loss of teeth Hallucinations

Prescription Stimulants (Adderall®, Ritalin®, Amphetamine)	Agitation Irritability Insomnia	Impaired thinking Seizure
Hallucinogens (LSD, Mushrooms, Ecstasy, MDMA)	Dehydration Anxiety Exaggerated affection for others	Teeth clenching Memory problems

RELATIONSHIPS

Substance use and addiction affect teenagers' family and social relationships by promoting lying, cheating, stealing, and general dishonesty. By definition, an addict must manipulate those around him. For instance, just to get their hands on illicit substances, teenagers—and not just addicted ones—commit illegal acts, and they might commit other crimes to raise money to buy their substance of choice. Teenagers also mislead their families and others who care about them so they can drink or use without intervention. Oftentimes, the addicted teenager will construct elaborate explanations for his perplexing behavior as a way to hide his compulsive substance use. If I had a nickel for every time I heard about a teenager telling his parents, "I was just holding the pot for a friend," I would be rich!

As often as substance misuse and addiction strain a teenager's relationship with his family, they also damage his relationships with peers. Many sexually promiscuous teenagers are mixed up with substances: using drugs and alcohol can put them in a vulnerable position or open the door to dangerous sexual behavior. Although the appropriateness of sexual behavior between teenagers is a family matter, promiscuous or otherwise damaging sexual behavior is always problematic at any age. Here, you as parents have a right and obligation to put your foot down; doing so can also present an opportunity to intervene in your teen's drinking or drug use.

Although drinking alcohol and using drugs often start out as communal experiences, teenagers who become addicted rapidly give up most of their friendships. The teenager who holes up in his room smoking pot isn't socializing anymore: He's abandoned his friends for his drug of choice. Similarly, the kid who's addicted to prescription opioids like Vicodin® often becomes so focused on keeping up a regular supply that his friendships become secondary to that goal. One young college student I treated took advantage of her high school friends, her boyfriend, and even her landlady, as ready sources of cash and rides to the spot where she bought her OxyContin®. Friends who feel used don't stick around for long. If you see this pattern with your teenager, trust your instincts and immediately confront him and get him into treatment.

Of course, social isolation and alienation from a peer group can promote drug use among teenagers—or anyone. For the teen in economic distress, lacking opportunities for engaging with others or participating in healthy activities, the temptations of drug and alcohol use can be overwhelming. Primary prevention modalities for teenagers involve promoting social engagement, engineering job opportunities, and "saving" the teen from endless empty after-school hours, all in the hope of discouraging substance use and other self-destructive behaviors.

Relationship problems can signal drug or alcohol problems, and are a perfect place to intervene. If your teenager screams at you, "The only reason my drinking is a problem is because you think it's a problem!" just accept that. It's a fine place to start, because you really don't care at this point why your teenager is misusing drugs and alcohol—you just want her to stop! Someday, with your guidance and support, your child will see it as a problem, too.

SCHOOL

Problems with school can be the first hints of substance use that a parent picks up—whether they surface in a call from a teacher, steadily dropping grades, or simply a lack of interest in classes and activities. However the problems come to light, they give parents and teachers the opportunity to help the substance-using teenager. For instance, if your child starts bringing home failing grades, immediately meet with teachers, counselors, coaches, and any other staff or faculty members who know her. They may or may not know anything about your teenager's addiction, but they'll be able to refer her to treatment centers and offer ongoing monitoring for alcohol and drug use. Even if your teenager's problem with grades is unrelated to her problem with substances, a school meeting can help you marshal resources for helping her.

Of course, when it comes to substance misuse, be aware that school personnel may have obligations beyond watching out for your teenager. School employees may be required to report to supervisors, or even to the police department, any suspicion of drug or alcohol use by a student. The school may also have policies for suspending substance-using students. Your teenager's use of substances may also undermine her Individualized Educational Plan (IEP), if she has one. Make sure you know the school policies before you meet with school personnel. A warning from her school might be just the catalyst you need to start getting some help.

Tough Talk Dialog: "The Teachers Just Hate Me!"

Bill: Anna, I got a call from the school counselor today.

Anna: I know, Dad, they told me they were going to call you. It's all bullshit what they're saying about me.

Bill: Well, maybe, but I need to know what's going on. I'm so worried about you.

Anna: There's nothing to be worried about.

Bill: Mrs. Pembroke said that you looked high and she saw pills in your purse when you opened it in class. The security guard said it was Ecstasy.

Anna: Oh Dad, you're so wrong. Those were just Motrin®. I have my period. It's none of their business what medications I take. This is so embarrassing!

Bill: Oh, come on sweetheart. They know and you know those weren't Motrin®. Motrin® doesn't make you high and

the school wouldn't be calling me if they weren't absolutely sure.

Anna: The teachers just hate me! That's why they're doing this
to me. They want to ruin my life.

Bill: Actually, Mrs. Pembroke sounded very worried about
you, but that's not the issue. The school is making a report, and you need to get drug tested and have an evaluation before you go back to class. We don't have a choice
on this.

Anna: Yes, we do! You can sue them! This is so unfair!

Bill: Well, I made an appointment with a drug counselor they
recommended, who can evaluate you and do the drug
testing. It's for tomorrow afternoon.

Anna: No way! (Crying) I'm not going. You can't make me!

Bill: We need to do this, sweetheart. It's mandatory from the
school. Whatever comes out of this, you'll be able to get
back on track.

Anna: I hate you!

Anna's father doesn't argue with her about whether or not she is
addicted, nor does he get sucked into the argument that her teachers
are hateful. He merely observes that the school thinks Anna has a
drug issue and is requiring a drug test and assessment. It's fine to
allow the school counselor to be the bad guy: The most important
thing is that Anna will be evaluated.

THE LAW

Another common way that parents find out their teenager is using
drugs or alcohol is through the legal system—that dreaded late-
night phone call from the precinct. It's natural to be worried and
frightened if your teenager gets into a mess with the police because
of her substance use, but it can be an illuminating experience as
well as inarguable evidence that she's struggling with drugs or alcohol. If there wasn't a problem, she wouldn't be getting arrested,
detained, or questioned by the police.

Law enforcement officers aren't always right and mistakes do sometimes occur, but an encounter with the cops or courts can be a springboard to getting your teenager some support. Enlightened police officers, prosecutors, and judges can often provide assistance. In fact, data gathered by the federal Drug and Alcohol Services Information System shows that most teenagers who are admitted to addiction treatment programs arrive there via the criminal justice system. Trouble with the law may turn out to be a very good thing!

Needless to say, one would always hope that a teenager would have no interaction with the police or the justice system, and certainly tragedies can result from overzealous police officers, or disturbed drug users, or even frank prejudice. Although no one wants their child to be arrested for using or selling drugs, it's far better that she be remanded to treatment at the age of fifteen than continue using. If she doesn't get treatment until she's older, she'll be more damaged by her addiction and will be unlikely to receive much understanding from the courts. I've noticed that prosecutors and judges almost invariably go out of their way to help teenagers who are mixed up with drugs and alcohol; this collaboration can be a tremendous advantage to a teenager and those who care about her.

DEFINING THE PROBLEM: WARNING BELLS

A wide range of behavior and situations can signal that your teenager is having difficulties with substance use or other compulsive behavior. For each of the items listed here, see the corresponding chapter and Appendix B: Readers' Resources for more information.

> **Substances in general (chapters 1-2):** poor school performance or skipping school (except stimulant medications)... acting out at school... abandonment of enjoyable activities... loss of friends... difficulties at work or missing work... need for excessive amounts of cash... lying, cheating, stealing... promiscuity or other dangerous sexual behavior... run-ins with the police... use of drug slang when speaking with friends (see Appendix A: Glossary of Selected Drug Terminology and Slang)

Alcohol (chapter 3): drunk driving... alcohol poisoning... sexual molestation (generally of girls)... involvement in fights (most often for boys)... use of other, more lethal drugs

Cigarettes (chapter 3): smoke on breath and clothes... hourly need to "take a walk"

Illicit stimulants (chapter 4): euphoria... irritability... impaired judgment... elevated blood pressure... change in overall energy level... weight loss... fixation on immediate gratification... bloody or painful nose (if snorted)... skin infections (if injected)... burned lips and fingertips (if smoked)... insomnia, then lethargy (withdrawal)... suicidal depression (withdrawal)

Marijuana (chapter 5): reddened eyes... lethargy... tendency to isolate... paranoia

Hallucinogens (chapter 5): glassy eyes... "checked-out" look... odd behavior

Opioids (chapter 6): episodes of overwhelming fatigue... falling asleep at odd times... taking daylong naps... impaired thinking... inability to comprehend conversations... drooping eyelids... constricted (pinprick) pupils

Benzodiazepines (chapter 6): lethargy... poor motivation... drooping eyes.

Stimulant medications (chapter 7): rapid and unexplained improvement in academic performance... abrupt weight loss... insomnia or ability to stay up all night... agitation

Steroids (chapter 7): rapid muscle growth... sudden increase in weight... significant improvement in athletic performance... facial acne... emotional instability... testicular shrinkage (in boys)... growth of facial hair (in girls)... growth of breast tissue (in boys)

Food, sex, and gambling in general (chapter 8): extreme eating, dieting, sexual behavior, or gambling... disproportionate focus on food, sex, or gambling

Food (chapter 8): continual talking about food and weight... severe or rapid weight loss... intense dieting or exercise... food or meal avoidance... binging... purging

Sex (chapter 8): multiple sexual partners... sexting (sending sexually explicit pictures or texts to others)... posting sexual images on social media sites... drug- or alcohol-fueled sexual behavior... exhibitionism... having sex in exchange for money, drugs, or other compensation

Gambling (chapter 8): preoccupation with gambling... gambling online or at high stakes... chasing losses with more bets... using lunch money or allowance to gamble

DENYING THE PROBLEM

Addicted teenagers will do almost anything to keep their parents— and themselves—from recognizing a problem. The most common smoke screen that teenagers (and others) use to avoid dealing with their substance use or addiction is denial, a psychological protection against painful or overwhelming feelings. In this case, such difficult emotions are those that accompany substance misuse. Denial can work in positive ways, too; denying the likely outcome of a terminal illness, for example, can allow a patient to maintain hope and keep fighting. Though in the case of addiction, denial is both destructive to the teenager and infuriating to those around him.

Sometimes a teenager will come into my office and tell me that he rarely uses marijuana and that his parents are just overreacting because they found him smoking his first joint with some friends.

As he's telling me this, my entire office is suffused by the smell of marijuana from his breath, clothes, and perhaps from the marijuana in his pocket. This may seem like lying—and certainly, addicted people do lie—but it's much more likely that the teenager really believes what he's telling me, that he doesn't use marijuana much. He doesn't recognize his problem. Denial explains why addicted teenagers can tell such unbelievable stories, which their parents often believe.

You may recognize your teenager's problem before he does. When faced with his denial, your best response is honesty: "Wow. You say that you don't smoke much marijuana, but I can smell it across the room." Combined with that honesty should be an understanding that your teenager genuinely doesn't realize how obvious his substance use is to others, that he may not be in control of his drug or alcohol habit, and certainly needs help. When talking the situation over with your teenager, it's best to go around his denial rather than bashing into it.

Tough Talk Dialog: "Maybe I Had a Sip of Beer."

Mr. Robinson:	*Hey Bobby, can I talk to you for a second?*
Bobby:	*Sure, Teach, what's up?*
Mr. Robinson:	*I saw you at the bonfire Friday night and I was a little worried about you.*
Bobby:	*Worried? Why?*
Mr. Robinson:	*Well, you looked drunk, kiddo. I hope you weren't driving.*
Bobby:	*No way! I wasn't even drinking. Some of the guys were, but I had to play on Saturday. There's no way I would drink and screw that up.*
Mr. Robinson:	*That makes sense, but you looked all glassy-eyed and you didn't even recognize me when I waved to you. I could see that you guys were passing around a bottle.*
Bobby:	*Maybe I had a sip of beer, but nothing more than that. I don't have any issues with alcohol!*

Mr. Robinson:	*I guess your memory of that's really different from mine. Since you mention it, how would you know you had a problem?*
Bobby:	*Well, I would definitely have a problem if I drank and then drove—I would never do that. If Coach found out I was drinking and benched me, that would be a huge problem for me. That's it, I guess.*
Mr. Robinson:	*OK, but you know that Coach could bench you or even kick you off the team for drinking just a sip of beer, right?*
Bobby:	*I guess so...*
Mr. Robinson:	*And you had a sip. Sounds like you've got an alcohol issue right now.*

Mr. Robinson says what he thinks, but doesn't hammer Bobby over the head with the obvious or get angry about the apparent lie. Rather, he gets Bobby to describe the potential problem. Once Bobby can put the problem into words, he's more likely to recognize that he has one.

COVERING UP FOR FRIENDS

Loyalty to friends is an important value that teenagers hold onto for dear life. Unfortunately, sometimes loyalty goes too far. You've probably discussed this with your child as she's grown up and it's extremely important that you define the acceptable limits of loyalty. While hoping that covering up for her friends will keep you from recognizing her problem, it also keeps her from recognizing it as well. Long before this potential situation, let your teenager know that while you respect and admire loyalty between friends, secrecy around drugs and alcohol can be deadly.

Probably the best way to gain your teenager's confidence concerning her loyalty to her friends is to react calmly to any news of substance misuse by your teenager or others in her circle. As the parent of teenagers, I know that fear is the natural first response when you hear about your little darling using drugs or alcohol. As a psychiatrist—it pains me to say it—this is a situation where you should hold those feelings in. Rather than freaking out in front of your teenager, vent with your spouse, close friend, or your therapist.

In this circumstance, try to approach your teenager as you would another adult whom you care about. Applaud her desire to remain loyal to friends, but treat her loyalty exactly as it is: an adult decision, with adult consequences. Ask her to ask herself, "If I remain silent about my friend's substance use and it gets worse, what's my responsibility? How will I feel? What if the addiction puts my friend in the hospital? Or she dies?" If you discuss the situation with your teenager as you would with an adult, she's more likely to make the right choice than if you demand she betray what she feels is a confidence.

EVERYONE DOES IT

Ah, the ultimate rationalization (see "Brooklyn Bridge, Jumping Off"). If everyone's doing it, it's not a problem! You've probably heard "everyone does it" innumerable times about innumerable subjects as your teenager has, quite naturally, been learning how to fit into society. No matter how we identify ourselves, we all want to fit in with our peers, at every age. Unfortunately, when your kid's "society" consists of boundary-pushing, booze-drinking, drug-using rebels, that's how he defines "everyone." He wants to hang with them, dress like them, and do what they do. No problem, right?

Wrong. "Everyone does it" is a refusal to recognize a problem and an attempt to convince you that there's no problem in the first place. When your teenager tries this tactic around substance use, take the opportunity to open a discussion. What's "everyone" doing? What's good about substance use? Has anyone he knows or has heard of been better off from doing alcohol or drugs, or just been hurt from doing them? Gone to rehab? What other choices is your teenager making because "everyone does it"? When you recognize a problem, a conversation like this can help your teenager recognize it too.

HOW PARENTS SHOULD REACT

Once you have recognized a problem and started a conversation with your teen, you may react in ways that are unhelpful—although totally understandable. To find out that your child, who you love and would give your life for, is endangering himself, or stealing from you, or wasting the advantages you have provided him with, would terrify and enrage most people.

Throughout this book, I suggest perfectly logical and well-researched options for treating a teen who misuses drugs or alcohol, but your teen is unlikely to access any of those treatments if you scream or cry or just "lose it" while trying to get him to that treatment!

Many, if not most, parents with a drug- or alcohol-using teen will need help in managing their child's problems *without* expressing those sorts of feelings. I'm certainly not saying that you shouldn't experience terror and anger about your son's drug use, only that you should handle it outside the room where you are trying to help your child. Going to a therapist to help you deal with your own feelings about the problem is often useful, not least because the therapist can assist you in focusing on the most relevant aspects of the problem, and giving you a place to express your (quite natural) frustration. Many outpatient and inpatient treatment facilities have family groups that are specifically tasked to rally the addicted person's loved ones in service of helping with recovery. Some well-defined outpatient therapy programs, such as *Community Reinforcement and Family Training* (CRAFT), and Dr. Marc Galanter's *Network Therapy* formally integrate the family into the treatment team, while helping loved ones manage their feelings in the most productive way possible. And Al-Anon, for the family members of addicted people, provides mutual support and examples of families and spouses who have helped an addicted person, while maintaining the necessary emotional distance from that person.

POINTS TO REMEMBER

- Give your teenager a clear and simple definition of alcohol and drug misuse and addiction.
- Use your definition to recognize problems as they arise.
- Deal with the health effects of drinking and drug use as soon as you see them.
- Turn relationship, school, and legal troubles into opportunities to recognize a problem and start treatment.

Denial is common in addiction: Go around it. Ask your teenager how he would feel if a friend he covered for died.

SECTION II:

SPECIFIC SUBSTANCES AND PROBLEMS

Chapter 3

ALCOHOL AND CIGARETTES

First you take a drink, then the drink takes a drink, then the drink takes you.

—F. Scott Fitzgerald (1896–1940)

Although you might prefer that your teenager never use alcohol, other drugs, or cigarettes, the statistical reality is that she will at least try them. Nonetheless, very few families demand that their children abstain completely from such substances. Each family must go with whatever policy their values dictate, what worked for the parents in their teenage years, and what they think is best for their teenager. You may find that one of your teenagers does well with a relatively permissive set of rules, while another needs much stricter limits.

While you may acknowledge the reality of teen alcohol and nicotine use, it's very important to try to delay it for as long as possible. In the case of alcohol, early use is associated with later problematic use. A study of college students who had a problem with alcohol, published in the journal *Substance Misuse* in 2008, found that those who had their first drink before the age of fourteen were much more likely—than their later-starting classmates—to drink more than twice a week, drink seven or more drinks in one sitting, and use alcohol in a self-destructive way. Similarly, for teenagers who try cigarettes, the later the better. As children grow up, their judgment improves, their susceptibility to peer pressure decreases, and their brains become less vulnerable to damage by toxins. Holding off on that first drink or cigarette as long as possible diminishes immediate harmful effects and makes eventual harmful use less likely.

HOW ABOUT A ZERO-TOLERANCE POLICY FOR ALCOHOL?

Zero tolerance for alcohol use by your twelve-year-old may be a perfectly viable plan, but establishing zero tolerance for your eighteen-year-old is probably not realistic (unless yours is one of the rare American families who fully abstain from alcohol). For most of us, zero tolerance for drinking by our fifteen- to eighteen-year-olds is almost impossible to enforce and defies common sense. A zero-tolerance policy will likely drive your teenager's alcohol use underground so you'll never hear about it, making it much tougher to get him help if he needs it.

What worries me even more, though, is that completely banning alcohol can undermine your attempts to ban other, more deadly, substances. If you melodramatically exaggerate and insist that any use of alcohol leads immediately to alcoholism, your teenager will know you're lying and therefore won't believe your similar arguments against heroin or cocaine. Aside from those who go with "zero tolerance," every parent reaches the point where he has to decide when to allow his teenager to experiment with alcohol. Teenagers must make the same decision and—trust me on this—their time frame is much earlier than yours!

Speaking with your teenager about your policy on drinking is an excellent chance to open a dialog with him about your feelings on the subject, what you can accept, what will cause you to worry, and what will make you forbid further alcohol use. Treating your teenager as a near-adult, with whom you're willing to have a reasonable discussion, should allow you to engage genuinely with him about his use of alcohol and other drugs. You don't have to agree with your teenager if he thinks experimenting with alcohol is a good idea, but if you acknowledge the reality that he and his friends are likely to drink, you can keep him safe, watch for signs of addiction, and generally stay in the game.

CHANCES ARE, YOUR TEENAGER WILL USE ALCOHOL

You're probably getting the idea that I think you should manage rather than absolutely bar alcohol use by your teenager. I do know some families who prohibit their teens from using alcohol and have good results, but most families don't absolutely prohibit alcohol use by their sixteen- to eighteen-year-olds. Regardless of what parents say, many teenagers use alcohol on a regular basis. According to a 2016 report from Monitoring the Future (an ongoing study of drug and alcohol use by teenagers and young adults), more than 22 percent of eighth graders, 43 percent of tenth graders, and 61 percent of twelfth graders had used alcohol at some point. More troubling, 8.6 percent of eighth graders, 26 percent of tenth graders, and 46 percent of twelfth graders said that they had been drunk.

Whatever you or I may think about it, we're pretty much left with trying to keep our children safe, rather than expecting them not to drink. It's the most realistic alternative. You might feel uneasy delivering what seems to be a mixed message to your teenager, but the best most of us can do is tell our kids that drinking alcohol at their age is a bad idea—not to mention illegal and dangerous—and set limits on their drinking rather than banning it altogether. Let your teenager know you're uncomfortable sending a mixed message and ask him how he feels about it. For older teenagers, this conversation may be a way to acknowledge their adult responsibilities and the difficulty of making adult decisions for which they're ultimately responsible.

Try to think of alcohol use the way you might think of teenage sexuality (which is often connected to drinking), STDs, and birth control. Although you most likely prefer that your teenager not be sexually active in middle and high school, you probably tell him to use a condom if he decides to have sex. For most parents, preventing pregnancy and sexually transmitted diseases is more important than taking a stand against teenage sexual behavior, in the same way that preventing harm from alcohol use is more important than preventing use of alcohol.

SHE'LL PROBABLY TRY CIGARETTES, TOO

In some ways, teenage cigarette smoking is similar to teenage drinking: it's illegal because of age restrictions, carries potential health risks, and is extremely common. The Center for Disease Control and Prevention has determined that cigarettes kill more Americans every year than alcohol, cocaine, and heroin put together. So, what's the best way to keep your teenager from smoking cigarettes (if you can) and to prevent addiction or long-term use if she experiments? First and foremost, don't smoke: If you don't smoke, your teenager is less likely to smoke. By setting an example and forbidding her to smoke in your home, cars, or presence, you underscore the fact that smoking is unhealthy, addictive, offensive to others, and just plain stupid.

Should you have a zero-tolerance policy? There's no good reason to let your teenager flirt with nicotine addiction, emphysema, and lung cancer. However, as with alcohol, a zero-tolerance policy generally isn't practical for families with teenagers over the age of fifteen or sixteen. A good alternative is to strongly counsel your teenager not to smoke, ban cigarettes in and around your home, and refuse to fund cigarette purchases.

A measured response to smoking reduces the chance that your teen will develop a nicotine addiction, and it opens the way for an aggressive approach to other substances that can kill your teenager on the spot, such as cocaine and heroin. It's hard to prove that cigarettes are a "gateway drug" that lead teenagers to use alcohol and other substances. For instance, there's no proof that nicotine addiction causes heroin addiction, but it's interesting to note that most heroin users start their substance misuse careers by smoking cigarettes. Bottom line, whether or not they're a gateway drug for your teenager, cigarettes are extremely addictive.

WHAT IF *YOU* USE ALCOHOL OR CIGARETTES?

If you use alcohol and cigarettes, you send your teenager the message that they're safe, enjoyable, and a mark of adulthood. If you drink only in moderation, you're probably setting a good and realistic example, since many American adults use alcohol safely without any negative consequences. Though with smoking—even if you suffer no immediate harm—you're almost inevitably setting up your smoking teenager for misery later on.

If either you or your teenager is addicted to alcohol, parental drinking is viciously counterproductive. A teenager with an alcoholic parent is more likely, on a genetic basis, to have an alcohol problem himself, and parents who have not dealt with their own problem and keep alcohol in the house create an unfair and obviously destructive temptation. The teenager will get the message that the alcohol drinking is OK and a fine way to live one's life, despite all evidence to the contrary. When a teenager with an alcohol issue comes into my office and says "my parents drink all the time," I know he's in for a rough ride. If his parents can't or won't clear their alcohol out of the house, the likelihood that he'll beat his problem plummets.

ASSESSING YOUR TEEN'S ALCOHOL USE

Since it's unlikely that we can entirely prevent our children from drinking, as parents we're left with assessing the risks and responding to them. You should consider your child's age: A fourteen-year-old getting trashed at a kegger is much different from a seventeen-year-old drinking a few cans of beer in a friend's backyard. Look also at any family history of alcoholism. If there is one, it's quite reasonable to take a different tack than if your family has never had alcohol issues. There's no one-size-fits-all standard: It's up to you to weigh the significance of your individual teenager's alcohol use and to determine if it fits your criteria for problem drinking or addiction.

If you acknowledge that your teenager is using alcohol, how can you tell when her drinking is an addiction? Certainly, any threat to her immediate safety suggests that she has a problem: By drinking too much, your teenager can endanger herself in many ways. It's absolutely necessary to ask her—and yourself—some scary questions about her behavior. If your teenager chimes any of the warning bells, you have serious cause for concern.

WARNING BELLS: ALCOHOL

- Drunk driving
- Drinking to the point of alcohol poisoning
- Using other drugs (which might be even more lethal)
- Victimization by a sexual predator
- Involvement in fights
- Abandonment of previously cherished activities or friends
- Alcohol-related contact with the police
- Difficulties with school or work

PREVENTING CAR ACCIDENTS

For every driver of any age, a zero-tolerance policy on driving while intoxicated (with alcohol or anything else) is a good, legally sound idea. Likewise, riding in a car with an intoxicated driver should be absolutely *verboten*. It's also wise to institute an "anywhere, anytime" plan for your teenager, so he can call you for a ride home if he's concerned about driving drunk, or about taking a ride with a drunk driver. That policy should come with your assurance that you won't get angry (at least for the time being). The vast majority of parents are willing to institute these guidelines. So why do so many teenagers die every year from alcohol-related car accidents?

I believe that it's because parents don't prepare very well for the drinking-and-driving scenario. Sometimes we don't address the issue because we're too circumspect and trusting with our teenagers, believing that our charming, obedient fifteen-year-old son would never do something so foolish. Or we wait too long to discuss it, not realizing that our eighth grader may be hanging out with older kids who have access to both alcohol and car keys. The takeaway is not to postpone that conversation about drunk driving or riding with impaired drivers, and to offer, early and often, to pick up your child at any place and time.

ALCOHOL POISONING AND ALCOHOL WITHDRAWAL

A drinker who rapidly consumes large amounts of alcohol will experience alcohol poisoning. Absolutely forbid your teenager from putting himself in situations where this might occur. Every September, newspapers publish obituaries of college freshmen who, as a part of a fraternity hazing or sorority initiation ritual, drank a bottle or more of hard liquor and died from respiratory depression (dramatically slowed breathing) or aspiration pneumonia that results when an intoxicated person inhales his own vomit.

These kids die because they haven't developed a tolerance for that much alcohol—their bodies don't break down the booze the way a more experienced drinker's would. A more experienced drinker would merely become intoxicated, and a confirmed alcoholic might show hardly any effects at all from drinking that much. Teenagers who experiment with drinking might take foolish risks with alcohol, so explain alcohol poisoning to your teen and unconditionally ban the kind of extremely dangerous drinking that can cause it. Get bothered about this one.

Alcohol withdrawal is what happens when a heavy drinker stops using alcohol or cuts down on his consumption. It causes confusion, elevated blood pressure and pulse, and eventually, hallucinations and tremors, which can progress to delirium tremens (seizure and sometimes death). Although rare among teenagers, this lethal syndrome warrants vigilance if your child drinks regularly. Anyone who shows any signs of alcohol withdrawal needs immediate medical attention.

In an unfortunate twist, the introduction to the United States of a beer called "Delirium Tremens," reflects our society's fascination with intoxicants and its blithe ignorance about their potential dangers. Delirium Tremens is a very popular beer made in the style known as Belgian strong pale ale and has an alcohol content of 8.5 percent, twice that of a conventional beer such as Budweiser or Coors. Do its fans know that *delirium tremens* kills thousands of Americans every year? Are they attracted by a name they think is clever and risqué? I doubt a fashionable brand of cigarettes would be named "Lung Cancer" or "Hacking Cough."

HOW DO I GET MY CHILD INTO ALCOHOL TREATMENT—AND KEEP HER THERE?

If you suspect that your teenager has an alcohol problem, it's time to throw out your acceptance of experimentation. You don't need to diagnose your child as an alcoholic; you need only notice that she has an issue with alcohol. When you do, tell her that you're seeing a problem—whether it's her difficulty in school, recurring drunkenness, failed friendships, or health troubles—then seek out a qualified addiction clinician and get your daughter an evaluation as soon as possible. (Chapter 10, "How to Find Good Treatment—and Get Your Teenager to It" explains how to get professional help.)

Finding treatment isn't your only obligation. If you think your teenager has an alcohol problem, stop drinking around her and get rid of any alcohol in the house. Let her know that you won't tolerate any further alcohol use and help her take the Alcoholics Anonymous step of changing her friends, hangouts, and interests. None of this is easy, but it's utterly necessary to support your teenager's sobriety and keep her in treatment. (More on this in chapters 10–13; also see Appendix B: Readers' Resources.)

CIGARETTES

Nicotine is a tremendously seductive and addictive drug, whether in the form of cigarettes, chewing tobacco, or snuff. Part of the reason is that the physical harm done by tobacco doesn't show up for decades. For the teenager who smokes, the possibility of getting lung cancer or emphysema in thirty or forty years is not particularly worrisome. Still, the evidence against tobacco is incontrovertible, and Americans have increasingly developed a strong bias against it over the last twenty years. With higher and higher taxes on cigarettes and bans on smoking in public places, governments have made it very inconvenient to smoke. Smoking is no longer as cool as it once was, but teenagers still face peer pressure to smoke, and many give in.

Any use of nicotine represents a potential problem, regardless of whether or not it's addictive, long-lasting, or frequent. Let your teenager know this, and if he develops a tobacco habit, help him find the abundant treatment that's available. Groups like Smokenders and Smokestoppers, sponsored by the American Lung Association, are helpful, as are Internet resources such as whyquit.com. In addition, there are several medications, including nicotine replacement patches and anti-craving drugs that your doctor can recommend.

POINTS TO REMEMBER

- The majority of teenagers experiment with alcohol and tobacco.
- Zero tolerance for drinking and smoking by your fifteen- to eighteen-year-old is rarely a viable strategy.
- Use discussions about setting limits as teachable moments.
- Warning bells for teenage alcohol misuse and addiction include difficulties at school, health problems, and frequent intoxication.
- If you think your teenager has an alcohol problem, seek help immediately!

Chapter 4

ILLEGAL STIMULANTS: COCAINE AND METHAMPHETAMINE

I like to keep a bottle of stimulant handy in case I see a snake,
which I also keep handy.

—W. C. Fields

Almost everyone knows how it feels to take a stimulant: Starbucks® is a money-making empire because they sell a legal stimulant, caffeine, not because they sell cookies. Coca-Cola® is the world's most valuable brand—among *all* brands, not just soft drink brands—not because it's got an eye-catching logo, but because Coke contains caffeine, the most popular of stimulants. Caffeine in moderate quantities—a cup or two of coffee or tea, or a can of soda—usually gives the user a short burst of energy, improved ability to concentrate, and mild euphoria. It can have a few unwelcome, but mild side effects, such as anxiety, irritability, and insomnia.

Alongside coffee, tea, and soda, are Red Bull® and countless other energy drinks. At your neighborhood convenience store, you'll see soft drinks that contain not only caffeine and sugar, but less recognizable natural substances derived from plants. One of those, guarana, packs about twice the caffeine of coffee. Taurine is another potent stimulant, and there are several others. The powerful stimulant and diuretic, ephedra, was banned by the federal government in 2004 after its use led to several deaths by dehydration. Weaker agents such as pseudoephedrine (found in Sudafed® and other cold remedies) mimic ephedra's effects and remain available over the counter for the treatment of the common cold. All of these stimulants are generally safe when not used to excess.

LEGAL VS. ILLEGAL STIMULANTS: WHAT'S THE DIFFERENCE?

Our society consumes a lot of caffeine in order to keep up with the demands of work and family. Many of us use it in moderate quantities to enhance mental alertness, fight fatigue, and generally boost our mood, effects that last around five hours. By drinking coffee every morning and perhaps, a caffeinated soda or energy drink in the afternoon, we can become dependent on caffeine, even if it sometimes makes us anxious, irritable, and sleep deprived.

Technically, this is an addiction, because we're using caffeine compulsively, despite its negative (if minor) side effects. If we're regular caffeine drinkers and we stop or decrease our daily intake, we might suffer withdrawal symptoms such as headaches and lethargy.

Caffeine's relative weakness as a stimulant and its usual mode of delivery—drinking a beverage—make it difficult to get too much. Caffeine intoxication certainly can occur, but the syndrome is relatively uncommon. With a lower tolerance than many adults, more teenagers than adults are at risk of overdosing themselves on caffeine. The effects—anxiety, agitation, headache, elevated blood pressure and pulse, and increased urination leading to dehydration—can last up to twelve hours. Although disconcerting and disruptive, they aren't usually dangerous. However, a massive overdose of caffeine can cause more serious symptoms and even death.

I'm not telling you to stop drinking coffee, but rather making the point that what you feel when you use caffeine hints at the much more rapid and powerful effects of the illicit stimulants that your teenager may be using. The stimulant properties of caffeine are much weaker than those of methamphetamine and cocaine, and its immediate and withdrawal effects are less severe than those of stronger stimulants. Just as caffeine drinkers seek increased energy and alertness, teenagers who don't find enough kick in caffeine turn to illegal stimulants to help them study. They oftentimes see success—for a while.

I've grouped the illegal stimulants together in one chapter because they have similar effects and withdrawal effects. (See Prescription Stimulants and Steroids in chapter 7 for information on legal stimulants such as ADD medications.) Right up front, I stress that **if your teenager is using illegal stimulants, it's a genuine medical emergency.** The drugs can be lethal, sometimes causing, for instance, heart attacks—even in young people who are using them for the first time. The potential dangers demand that your teenager is immediately evaluated to find out where he falls on the spectrum of use. Your stimulant-using teenager needs treatment right away!

WHAT STIMULANTS DO

All stimulants raise the level of the neurotransmitter dopamine in the brain, which improves concentration and mood. Increase dopamine a little (caffeine) and you get mild euphoria. Increase dopamine a lot (cocaine) and you get wildly grandiose fantasies, giddiness, sexual acting out, irritability, agitation, and rapid heartbeat (which can lead to heart attack). Another result of using any stimulant is the "crash" afterwards, which for coffee drinkers usually consists of tiredness, slowed thinking, and even mild sadness. For those withdrawing from cocaine and methamphetamine, the crash brings on suicidal depression, irritability, insomnia, and a powerful craving for more drugs.

The main difference between cocaine and methamphetamine is the time it takes for the drugs to take effect. Powder cocaine, usually snorted, has a very quick effect, but crack cocaine delivers an even faster and stronger high, since the cocaine vapors that are inhaled immediately send the drug into the brain. Methamphetamine that's smoked also causes immediate intoxication, but its effects are somewhat different and last longer. If you believe your teenager is using illegal stimulants, there are a lot of signs to watch for.

BATH SALTS

The substances marketed to teens as "Bath Salts" in head shops and gas stations are not bath salts at all—they have nothing to do with taking a quiet bubble bath. Rather, these illicit designer drugs, sometimes sold with calming names like "Ivory Wave," or "Bliss," contain stimulants like mephedrone and methylone, and cause agitation, hallucinations, paranoia, and suicidal behavior. Although the DEA, in 2012, banned the twenty-six most common substances marketed as bath salts, copycat manufacturers have produced other substances which, although not technically illegal, cause the same effects. The message is that your teen should not be buying anything at a gas station to snort into his nose—these stimulants can be deadly, and they are totally unregulated.

WARNING BELLS: ILLEGAL STIMULANTS

- Euphoria
- Irritability
- Impaired judgment
- Elevated blood pressure
- Change in overall energy level
- Weight loss
- Excessive need for money
- Fixation on immediate gratification
- Bloody or painful nose (if snorted)
- Skin infections (if injected)
- Burned lips and fingertips (if smoked)
- Insomnia, then lethargy (withdrawal)
- Suicidal depression (withdrawal)
- Craving for more stimulants (withdrawal)

Alert to these warning bells, one parent told me that she first realized her daughter was using cocaine when Lindsey became jittery about money. It became obvious when Lindsey asked her mom for money to go to the mall and seemed incapable of waiting even thirty seconds for her to get her purse from the closet. Lindsey followed her down the short hallway and into the coat closet(!), all the while loudly encouraging her to get the money quickly. Her mother thought to herself "What's wrong with this girl?" and recalled a recent phone call from Lindsey's lacrosse coach. The coach had told her of his own suspicions, but they had agreed that Lindsey was "too good of a kid to be using cocaine." The warning bells indicated otherwise.

HOW DO TEENAGERS TAKE STIMULANTS?

From snorting cocaine to overdosing on energy drinks, teenagers get their stimulant hits in a variety of ways. How your teenager takes an illegal stimulant influences how quickly he'll feel its effects. Teenagers snort powdered stimulants, rub them onto their lips or gums, smoke them, or inject them into a vein or under the skin. Powder cocaine is usually snorted through a tube and takes effect quickly, while smoking crack cocaine delivers an even faster and stronger high, since the cocaine vapors are immediately passed into the brain after being inhaled. Injecting a stimulant into a vein or under the skin also sends the drugs into the bloodstream much more rapidly than does swallowing a pill. Newer designer drugs like Flakka, a homemade amphetamine-like stimulant, can quickly provoke bizarre and hyperactive behavior.

Methods of Taking Illegal Stimulants

Stimulant	Method	Approximate Length of Effects
"Bath Salts"	Snorting	3-8 hours
Cocaine, powdered	Snorted, intravenous, injected under the skin, spread on gums or lips	2-4 hours
Crack cocaine	Smoked	1-2 hours
Methamphetamine pills (Desoxyn®)	Oral	2-6 hours
Methamphetamine rocks (crystal meth, ice, crank)	Smoked	2-24 hours

COCAINE 101

Lab rats will self-administer cocaine until they die. Unfortunately, so will some humans. In particular, crack cocaine (so named because of the snapping and crackling sound the rocks make when they're smoked) has instantly and intensely euphoric effects on the body and mind. This addictive high drives many users to abandon their livelihoods, families, and sense of self-worth in search of the next hit. I consider the use of cocaine in any form a true emergency, given that it can induce heart attacks: A user can drop dead the first time she uses cocaine! Talk to your teenager as soon as you suspect she's abusing any type of cocaine. When you do, hold back your own terror and tackle your daughter's mind-numbingly obvious denial of her cocaine use:

Tough Talk Dialog: "I Was Just Holding Chrissy's Cocaine."

Dad:	*Sandra, I came home from work so Mom and I could talk to you together. What's this all about?*
Sandra:	*Dad, I was just holding something for a friend ... and I got in a little trouble.*
Mom:	*A little trouble? The counselor said that you're suspended from school, you have to see a drug counselor and get drug tested, and they're thinking about calling the police! You had cocaine, for God's sake!*
Dad:	*Whoa. What's Mom talking about? You had cocaine?*
Sandra:	*Well, not really. I was holding Chrissy's. It was just until after school so if they checked her locker they wouldn't find it.*
Mom:	*So that's just great, they found it in your purse, not in Chrissy's locker. Did Chrissy back you up that it was hers? Or is she going to cut you loose on this?*
Dad:	*Well, whatever Chrissy's deal is, I'm more worried about you. Were you using the cocaine?*
Sandra:	*No! I wouldn't use that stuff. You know that!*
Dad:	*I don't really know that. You've lost a lot of weight lately. You seem a bit jumpy and your judgment is way off. I would never expect this of you.*

Sandra:	No *way. I wouldn't do that. I've just been doing more conditioning like coach told me to. My judgment is fine, what do you mean?*
Mom:	*What does Dad mean? He means that you were foolish enough to hold someone else's cocaine, even if it was for Chrissy. The police call that "possession," not doing someone a favor.*
Sandra:	*Are you kidding, Mom? One little mistake and you're all over me? What about Chrissy? It was her stuff!*
Dad:	*Frankly, we don't much care about Chrissy. We care about you. I will personally take you to that counselor and to get tested!*
Sandra:	*This isn't fair! I didn't do anything.*
Mom:	*Dad's right. We're going to get you some help for this.*

In this dialog, Sandra's parents clearly don't believe that she was "just holding" the cocaine, but they don't get hung up on that, or on Chrissy. They focus in on their main concern, Sandra's well-being, and insist on getting her help. They know that Sandra's use of cocaine could kill her on the spot or greatly shorten her life span—even to a few weeks or months. *Any* cocaine use can be deadly!

METHAMPHETAMINE 101

Methamphetamine, at least in its smoked form, is a special case among the illegal stimulants. It isn't that cocaine is benign—I've seen it destroy teenagers' lives—but the devastating consequences of smoked methamphetamine use strike me as exponentially more horrific than the evils of powder cocaine. Smoked methamphetamine delivers a very long-lasting high and has an especially all-encompassing impact on the user and his family. It's enormously difficult to get methamphetamine users into treatment and to help them stay sober. Yet, methamphetamine is readily available and affordable because it's both easy and cheap to produce.

Like most of the other stimulants, methamphetamine in pill form has some legitimate uses, for instance the treatment of narcolepsy, ADD, and (arguably) obesity. However "crystal meth," or "ice," smoking seems to have a particularly "sticky" effect on the lives of users, whose scarred and toothless faces have become familiar to Americans from the before and after pictures published by law enforcement. Once most prevalent among gay men on the West Coast and then teenagers in the middle of the country, smoked methamphetamine is now also widespread on the eastern seaboard and is used by all demographic groups.

If your child smokes methamphetamine, however, there's no reason to lose hope and there's every reason to get help NOW. Some treatments are quite effective in helping meth users. The best strategy is inpatient treatment, where professionals can use medications and relapse-prevention psychotherapy to deal aggressively with withdrawal symptoms like insomnia, depression, and craving. Researchers have also proposed using certain medications to reduce methamphetamine craving and withdrawal. Methamphetamine is a scourge, but you and your teenager can beat it!

POINTS TO REMEMBER
- All stimulants can cause agitation, irritability, and insomnia.
- Snorting or shooting medications is ALWAYS a danger sign.
- Cocaine use is a true medical emergency.
- Smokable methamphetamine is the most devastating stimulant drug.

Chapter 5

MARIJUANA AND OTHER HALLUCINOGENS

Pot didn't kill my son ... it just slowed him down.

—Parent, anonymous

Marijuana, the illegal drug most commonly used by teenagers, is widely accepted as harmless, but is it? Its effects range from the trivial—silliness, bloodshot eyes, etc.—all the way to catastrophic—paranoia, depression, and more. Many teenagers and parents don't realize that although not as potent, it's a hallucinogen similar to LSD and Ecstasy. Marijuana and the other hallucinogens can cause serious problems for teenagers who use them: The drugs can make them hear and see potentially dangerous things that aren't there, and can loosen or completely wipe out the user's grip on reality.

MARIJUANA 101

Each year, Monitoring the Future (MTF, www.monitoringthefuture. org) surveys high school students about their use of and attitudes toward various illicit substances. In 2016, the researchers surveyed 41,600 students in 377 high schools and found that more than 44 percent of twelfth graders acknowledged using marijuana at some point in their lives. This estimate is probably low, since it only reflects the percentage of kids who actually *admitted* that they used marijuana. Plus, the heavy marijuana users probably weren't even in school to be interviewed! Despite worries about trends in state laws decriminalizing medical or recreational marijuana use, monitoring the Future's statistics show a plateau, and perhaps a decrease, in teen marijuana use over the past three years.

Marijuana comes from the cannabis sativa plant, which contains a hallucinogenic chemical called tetrahyrdrocannibinol (THC). It goes by many names, including "pot," and the many others listed in the appendix to this book. Users smoke a combination of the plant's dried leaves and flowers; sinsemilla, a seedless variety, is especially potent. Hashish, typically called "hash," is dried cannabis resin and is also extra potent. Teenagers can smoke either form of cannabis in a joint or in a water pipe called a bong, which cools down the smoke so they can hold it in their lungs longer, amplifying the drug's effects. Another popular way to consume marijuana is to bake it into brownies or other sweets.

However it's used, marijuana normally causes symptoms such as silliness, difficulty walking, bloodshot eyes, and memory problems. Taken heavily or recurrently over a long period of time, marijuana can bring about paranoia, lack of motivation, depression, and profound fatigue. It's fairly easy to spot a teenage marijuana user.

WARNING BELLS: MARIJUANA
- Reddened eyes
- Lethargy
- Poor school performance
- Tendency to isolate
- Paranoia

GATEWAY DRUG, MEDICINE, OR JUST A HIGH?
You've heard a lot of talk about what marijuana is and is not. Some people claim that it's a "gateway" to harder drugs, and a lot of teenagers agree. While it's true that almost all users of hard drugs first

used marijuana, alcohol, and cigarettes, we can't say that those substances are to blame for their leap to harder drugs. Whether or not marijuana use influences later drug use, it's certainly true that kids who try marijuana at a young age have an attitude toward drugs that might point toward future trouble. Monitoring the Future research in 2016 shows that 58 percent of eighth graders think smoking marijuana regularly is risky—but that means 42 percent see no great risk. Between 2008 and 2016 there was a marked decrease in the risk that eighth graders attached to regular marijuana use.

If your teenager uses marijuana, it is indeed a risk factor for progressing on to other drugs, but that outcome isn't a sure thing. Don't panic! The vast majority of teenagers who use marijuana or alcohol never have serious trouble with either, nor do they move on to other substances. I don't mean to minimize the dangers of marijuana use, only to encourage you to look at these dangers realistically. You're better off ignoring the gateway drug question when deciding how to help your teenager. Of more concern is the harm marijuana might be doing to your teenager right now and the possibility that he's knowingly or unknowingly taking other drugs that might be added to the marijuana.

Some people look at marijuana from the opposite point of view, claiming that it's a valuable remedy for various health problems. Marijuana probably does have some medical benefits, but there's no good evidence that they outweigh its risks. California, one of the states that have legalized medical marijuana, even allows people with minor complaints—such as difficulty sleeping—to obtain marijuana legally through a network of licensed growers and vendors. And, as of March of 2017, eight states and the District of Columbia have made recreational marijuana use legal for those over the age of eighteen. In fact, in all fifty states, physicians can legally prescribe pharmaceutical grade THC (Marinol® and Cesamet®), the active ingredient in marijuana.

However, federal law prohibits the sale and possession of marijuana, and the federal government may well challenge medical and recreational marijuana laws at the state level. Patient advocacy groups and others are pushing for the legalization of marijuana on the state and national level, but *no* responsible party is in favor of making marijuana legally available to minors. This is another debate you don't need to have with your marijuana-using teenager!

IS THERE SUCH A THING AS MARIJUANA WITHDRAWAL?

Short answer: Yes! Anyone who tells you that quitting marijuana is no sweat is misinformed: Withdrawal produces a whole host of symptoms, including irritability and difficulties with sleep. Numerous scientific studies over the past fifteen years have authoritatively identified the medical phenomenon of marijuana withdrawal, and have shown its similarities to withdrawal from substances like alcohol, cocaine, and heroin. The 2013 edition of the Diagnostic and Statistical Manual (DSM) used by mental health professionals has added marijuana withdrawal to the list of other drug withdrawal syndromes.

Even so, some marijuana users doubt the reality of withdrawal. Sure, it's no fun to stop smoking, and the uncomfortable symptoms may explain why your teenager keeps going back to marijuana after he's stopped using it. He thinks it's the marijuana that makes him feel better, but, in fact, his relief stems from coming out of withdrawal.

SYMPTOMS OF MARIJUANA WITHDRAWAL

- Insomnia
- Irritability
- Anxiety
- Decreased appetite
- Mood Swings
- Increased aggression/anger

The most important thing about marijuana withdrawal is that it can be treated. Although not physically dangerous, the symptoms of withdrawal should be managed to improve your teenager's chances of kicking the habit. An experienced physician can prescribe medication to minimize the physical misery of withdrawal while convincing your teenager that his symptoms will fade away and teaching him self-soothing strategies for dealing with his discomfort. Once he realizes that his doctor understands his symptoms and can treat them, and that they will disappear with time, he'll probably be able to tolerate withdrawal more easily.

YOUR BEST COURSE OF ACTION

If you discover that your teenager uses marijuana, I have three main pieces of advice for you. First, take a deep breath and count to ten. I mean this quite literally. You need to take in the fact that your darling child, whom you love, whom you've nurtured and protected, has been using an illegal substance in direct defiance of your rules and her own promise to abide by those rules. Not good. This is a very valuable moment to give yourself a time-out, so that you can step back and orient yourself to the task at hand: finding out what's going on and helping your teenager. It also gives you and your spouse or partner a chance to put your heads together and figure out how to respond; two heads are better than one in a crisis.

My second recommendation is that you start asking questions. Remember that your teenager isn't the enemy—her drug problem is. Don't lecture her or exaggerate the risks of marijuana use; that's just as unhelpful as minimizing its downsides. Resist the urge to vent your (understandable) anger: it will probably push her toward using more marijuana and for the time being, ruin your chances of protecting or at least helping her. Be careful how you ask your teenager about her marijuana use. Criticizing her in the guise of a question is a bad idea: "How could you be so stupid as to use drugs?" isn't a question, it's an attack. You'll have to do what therapists do, which is to ask questions designed to be as neutral as possible.

Tough Talk Dialog: "What? You Were Smoking Pot?"
Sally: *Mom, I've got to tell you something before dinner.*
Anna: *What is it?*
Sally: *Julie's mom is going to call you tonight—she caught us doing something we weren't supposed to be doing.*

Anna: *She did?*

Sally: *Promise you won't be mad?*

Anna: *I'll try, sweetheart. What happened?*

Sally: *Well ... we were in the garage and she saw us smoking some stuff.*

Anna: *Stuff? What kind of stuff?*

Sally: *I don't know... it might have been pot.*

Anna: *WHAT? YOU WERE SMOKING POT?*

Sally: *See! I knew you'd get mad!*

Anna: *Just give me a minute. (She pours herself a glass of water and starts drinking it.)*

Sally: *Are you mad?*

Anna: *I am, but I'm glad you're telling me this. I'm going to try and stay calm here.*

Sally: *We never did it before.*

Anna: *Oh, Sally, I will try to stay calm, but please tell me the truth. Remember last summer when you smelled like pot after the graduation party? When Dad and I asked you about it but you said you didn't know what we were talking about?*

Sally: *Yeah... maybe I tried it then.*

Anna: *OK, so you've been smoking pot for a while?*

Sally: *The way you say it, it sounds like I do it all the time, every day. I don't. Sometimes on weekends, we just fool around with it, like you and Dad have a glass of wine. You won't tell Dad about this, will you? He'll go nuts!*

Anna: *Yes, I will. Dad and I don't keep secrets, but let me handle Dad. Just be honest with us, so we can try to figure things out and see what to do. We're a family and we deal with problems together. I really appreciate your telling me about this—but I need to know what else you're doing, sweetheart.*

Anna doesn't focus on Sally's previous lie or the fact that she's only coming clean because she has to—a call is coming in that evening from Julie's mother. There's no need to point out the obvious, since it would simply drive Sally into a defensive silence. Anna doesn't agree to keep the secret from her husband—addictions thrive on secrecy—but she promises to try to manage his reaction.

My third piece of advice about responding to your teenager's marijuana use is to set logical consequences for her behavior. In his book, *Choices & Consequences: What to Do When a Teenager Uses Alcohol/Drugs: A Step-by-Step System That Really Works,* addiction counselor Dick Schaefer explains what this means and distinguishes between natural and logical consequences. Natural consequences are those that teenagers experience as a result of their own behavior, without the involvement of friends or family. These could include nosebleeds from snorting cocaine, arrests for driving while intoxicated, or being suspended from school for drug use. Logical consequences, by contrast, are those that a teenager's loved ones establish in hopes of maintaining her safety, encouraging change, and promoting treatment.

Logical consequences can have a great impact on your teenager, so be careful when you put them in place. Some good examples are grounding your teenager if her urine toxicology test is positive (or if she refuses to take one) or withholding her allowance if she smokes pot. These are well-chosen, logical consequences: They're proportionate to her behavior, directly tied to her substance use, set up in advance, and easily enforceable. Logical consequences like these convince many teenagers to seek treatment, and are a mainstay of most early-phase addiction treatment programs.

HALLUCINOGENS 101

Like marijuana, other hallucinogens distort your teenager's perception of reality, but they're more potent than marijuana. This, most likely, is why teenagers generally enjoy them occasionally as opposed to every day, as they might marijuana. According to Monitoring the Future, 4.3 percent of high school students used a hallucinogen other than marijuana in 2014.

MDMA (ECSTASY, X)

MDMA (Methylenedioxymethampetamine), often called Ecstasy or X, is a "designer drug" concocted by scientists with the sole intention of making a new drug of abuse. It's not only a hallucinogen, but also a stimulant. Used by teenagers when they get together, the drug intensifies feelings of warmth toward others, reduces anxiety, and produces a general sense of well-being. Combined with these reactions, Ecstasy's stimulant effects can fuel hour upon hour of dancing. If a user fails to drink enough water, the result can be disastrous dehydration—even to the point of death. Heavy or frequent Ecstasy users can also experience significant memory loss. Although Ecstasy use by twelfth graders has decreased over the past two years, according to the MTF, 5 percent of twelfth graders acknowledge having used it. If your teenager uses Ecstasy, he'll likely tell you that it's a harmless party drug that he only does occasionally. As with all drugs, that's a bit like saying it's safe to play Russian roulette, since you haven't yet blown your brains out all over the floor—"yet" being the operative word. Make sure your teenager knows the dangers of using Ecstasy: In addition to the possibility of death by dehydration, he risks memory loss. When high on Ecstasy, his judgment might become so diminished that he does something destructive. Plus, he might actually be getting another drug when he buys Ecstasy illegally.

LSD

LSD (Lysergic acid diethylamide), commonly known as acid, was the first synthetic hallucinogen and has been used experimentally in military interrogations and in the treatment of terminally ill patients. It's officially classified as a Schedule I drug with no therapeutic value, and ever since 1967, when psychologist and author Timothy Leary told his generation to "turn on, tune in, and drop out," LSD has been a recreational drug—a drug of abuse. Usually, it's infused into small strips of paper and taken by placing the strips under the tongue. An effective dose is very small, so LSD is almost impossible to detect via drug testing. Being that it's manufactured under the table, dosing is uncontrolled: Your teenager never knows exactly how much she's getting in a hit.

The power of acid to induce weird cognitive distortions (the "trip") continues to fascinate teenagers. These hallucinations may be interesting or fun, but they can also terrify the user, who might do dangerous things in an attempt to escape horrible illusions. One common long-term effect—flashbacks—can occur weeks, months, and sometimes years after the user's original trip. While lasting only a short time, such flashbacks can be disorienting and scary. Visual trails (seeing lights trail after objects moving in front of you) are another common phenomenon. As with other hallucinogens, using acid can plunge your teenager into serious mental illness, though there's no proof that the drug actually causes this. Fewer and fewer teenagers are using LSD—2.4 percent in 2014, compared with 7.2 percent in 2000—but parents should be on the alert for warning signs.

SALVIA, "K-2," AND OTHER MARIJUANA SUBSTITUTES

Teenagers take salvia—the seeds, leaves, or liquid extract of the salvia dinorum plant—for its hallucinogenic properties. It's also perfectly legal in most states. About five or ten minutes after it's chewed (more quickly if it's inhaled or smoked), salvia causes visual distortions, a sense of disconnection from reality and distinct silliness. Popular YouTube videos illustrate what they claim are salvia's effects: One titled, "Salvia Trip" (www.youtube.com/watch?v=RmPfj_4uqHQ) has been viewed more than 1.8 million times. The video shows an intoxicated teenager who's supposedly taken salvia; she's giddy, has perceptual distortions, and a facial tic. If your teenager is using salvia, focus on preventing any potential harm. The questionable composition of salvia preparations, which might include other drugs, poses a real danger.

Salvia has recently been joined by a variety of substances with similar effects, such as "Spice" and "K2," illegal since March of 2010. Current drug tests can't detect them, but new tests are in development. The synthetic marijuana-like drugs "Spice" and "K2" are both unregulated and unsafe, yet drug dealers will continue to roll out new hallucinogens expressly to avoid detection by standard drug testing.

KETAMINE (K) AND PCP (PHENCYCLIDINE)

Powerful hallucinogenic drugs, ketamine and PCP cause disorientation and impaired thinking. Intoxication with PCP especially can set off violent outbursts that can last for hours, and teenagers sometimes end up taking massive overdoses, bringing on quite dangerous highs. Used in pill, powder, or liquid form, ketamine and PCP are often sprinkled on marijuana cigarettes or poured into drinks, sometimes unbeknownst to the smoker or drinker. Teenagers who take either of these hallucinogens take their lives in their hands. Although there are some emerging research studies about using ketamine in the process of psychotherapy, this research is about giving precise dosages of ketamine to adults with specific psychiatric problems, in a highly monitored and structured research program. Notwithstanding these studies, any teenager's use of ketamine and PCP is like a problem: Get help immediately!

MAGIC MUSHROOMS

Mushrooms containing psilocybin have been used for thousands of years to change consciousness and psychotherapeutic reasons. Although these mushrooms are indeed natural, they can still cause frightening episodes for the teens that use them, and a pattern of persistent and compulsive use, which can draw the teen away from participating in everyday life. In the worst scenario, the teen can experience long-lasting, intrusive, and frightening visual hallucinations. As with all illicitly obtained substances, the content, potency, and additives in Magic Mushrooms are all impossible to quanitify and therefore dangerous for the user.

INHALANTS

Teens can snort (huff) vaporized chemicals as varied as the aerosol sprays used to clean computer keyboards, to glue, to amyl nitrate, to kerosene, all in an effort to change consciousness. Unfortunately this change can result in serious mouth and nose damage, paralysis, impaired thinking, and, over time, loss of muscle mass. Given the wide range of potentially dangerous agents in this category, you should have a very low bar for suspecting drug use if you notice your teen buying or using more than minimal quantities of even common household materials like Dust-Off©, spray whipped cream, or lighter fluid.

TALKING TO YOUR HALLUCINOGEN-USING TEENAGER

From one perspective, a teenager who uses hallucinogens is doing exactly what a young person is supposed to do: expanding his thinking, opening up to new experiences, taking chances, etc. Though as their parent, you're obligated to help your teenager assess the risks and benefits of the chances he's taking and to guide him in keeping his experiments within safe bounds. Don't hesitate to use your own life experiences, whether with drugs or with other situations, to frame your own thinking and teach your teenager about gambling with his safety. Be careful, however, not to get sidetracked by arguments about your own history. Your teenager will almost certainly tell you that your ideas don't apply, but they do—and he knows it. You'll have to persevere in the face of almost certain disrespect, but your words will be heard despite the eye-rolling.

Tough Talk Dialog: "But You Did Drugs, Dad!"

Ed: So, Sammy, Mom told me that you were pretty whacked out when you came home last night.

Sam: I wasn't on anything, Dad. I was just tired—it was four in the morning!

Ed: Please, Sam, Mom knows tired and she knows high. You were tripping and looked scared out of your mind, and she didn't smell any pot. Susan said you had taken an LSD tab and were worried that you couldn't come down.

Sam: Well...

Ed: *I'm not even asking you if you took the acid, since it's pretty obvious. I just want to know if you're OK now and how we can help you stop.*

Sam: *I'm fine. Maybe I don't need to stop. You told me what you did in college. You and Mom tried LSD—that's how you know what a bad trip is!*

Ed: *You're right, I did drop acid and it was not a good thing for me, either. I wish I hadn't. The two times I did it were really unpleasant and I never did it again.*

Sam: *If you did it, why can't I?*

Ed: *First, I'm not going to allow you to use drugs, unfair as that may seem to you. Secondly, I want you to learn from my bad experiences—I also broke my ankle that year, but that doesn't mean you should, too! I love you and I don't want any harm to come to you.*

Sam: *This isn't fair.*

Ed: *Well, maybe not, but the hard and fast rule here is NO DRUGS. Period. I know you and your friends do a lot of great stuff that has nothing to do with drugs. Mom and I don't want to see all of that—or you—get messed up.*

Sam: *It wasn't that great, anyway. I don't think I even want to try it again.*

Ed: *Smart move. If anyone offers you drugs again, blame it on me and Mom when you turn them down.*

Ed doesn't allow the conversation to turn into a debate about the LSD he and his wife used in college. He acknowledges Sam's point, but nonetheless takes on the parental duty of establishing boundaries. When it comes to drugs, it's right for parents to set limits. Admittedly, it's a paradoxical and complicated position: Ed forbids Sam to use drugs, but nonetheless wants him to come to him if he does break the rules. Whatever Sam does, he knows his parents won't tolerate any drug use.

Ed's decision to acknowledge his past experimentation with drugs is not an easy one. It would have been perfectly reasonable to refuse to discuss it, since there are plenty of things that he and his wife rightly don't discuss with Sam, their sex life being one obvious example. Ed's decision to self-disclose his drug use was probably a good one, since it helped him steer the conversation toward drugs and their dangers. You'll have to decide how much you disclose to your teen about your own substance use; whatever you decide, don't let him deflect your drug discussions into convoluted squabbles about who did what. It just doesn't matter that much.

POINTS TO REMEMBER

- Marijuana is an addictive hallucinogen.
- Marijuana withdrawal causes irritability, anxiety, and insomnia.
- Don't overreact—or underreact—to your teenager's use of marijuana. Step back, ask questions, and set logical consequences.
- Hallucinogens can be lethal. Get help as soon as you learn that your teenager is using them.
- If your teenager asks if you have ever taken hallucinogens or other drugs, use the question as a teachable moment.

Chapter 6

SEDATIVES: OPIOIDS AND BENZODIAZEPINES

They don't call it "dope" because it makes you smarter...

—Anonymous

Sure, we all experience occasional pain—when our tennis elbow acts up, for instance—and sometimes we find it difficult to shed the stresses of our hyper-busy, demanding lives. It's at times like these that we take an aspirin or drink a glass of wine. Once in a while, though, we need a little extra help, and that's when our doctors might prescribe an opioid like codeine or a benzodiazepine like Klonopin®. Unfortunately, the very same effects that make these sedatives useful attract teenagers who are in search of a blissful, relaxing high that offers emotional escape. Also unfortunately, teenagers can easily and quickly become addicted to these drugs.

OPIOIDS 101

The sharp increase in opioid-related deaths in the last ten years has led to numerous government efforts to decrease the availability of prescription opioids like Vicodin®, Percocet®, and OxyContin®. Unfortunately, addicted teens have migrated to the less expensive and now-easier-to-obtain heroin, which is so potent that it can be snorted rather than injected. The high risk of opioid-related overdose and death among teens that use them necessitates early and aggressive responses from those who care about the teen.

Derived from the opium poppy plant, the opioids take many forms, including heroin. I collectively refer to this assortment of drugs as "the opioids" because they have similar effects, even though some are more potent and last longer than others. (Technically speaking, *opiates* are drugs made from opium, and *opioids* are synthetically constructed drugs designed to cause the same effect, but for simplicity I will call the entire class of drugs "opioids.") Unlike many other substances of abuse, the opioids have legitimate and necessary medical uses, such as pain control after a bone break, easing discomforts during cancer treatments, or relief after a minor surgical procedure. In addition, some of the opioids—buprenorphine (Suboxone®) and methadone—can be used to treat addiction. (Opioids to treat opioid addiction? I'll get to that later.)

Although physicians and dentists often prescribe opioids, many teenagers seek them out by other means because of the sedated sense of well-being and calm—the high—that the drugs can create. However, the opioids carry a very real risk of physical dependence, and misuse can become problematic and even life threatening. Prescription by a doctor is a common route by which many adults become addicted, and teenagers are no less vulnerable to this phenomenon, called "medical addiction." The teen may be prescribed an opioid for a perfectly reasonable indication, like a broken bone, or after surgery, and then become addicted. A small percentage of human beings prescribed opioids will become addicted, but if your teen is the one, the prevalence in your family is 100 percent! For this reason, teens—or in fact anyone—should be conservative about using opioid medications for even legitimate indications. There are certainly medical situations where opioids are the treatment of choice, but those situations are relatively rare for teenagers. However, most teenagers who get addicted start by experimenting with pills they find in their parents' medicine cabinet or get from a friend. Addicts lose their ability to stop using the opioids despite very obvious negative consequences, and if they do stop using, they'll go through withdrawal. A particularly vicious new opioid variant has the street name "Krokodil," for the brown, ulcerated skin of those who inject this potent and short-acting drug. The anesthetic fentanyl is one hundred times more potent than morphine, and carfentanil is one hundred times more potent than that! When drug dealers cut their heroin with either of these substances, causing opioid-overdose deaths, they—perversely—enhance their own standing in the marketplace because they are evidently selling high-quality merchandise.

If your teenager's using any of the opioids, you'll probably see a number of side effects. The most marked are lethargy and slowed thinking. If your child falls asleep at dinner or "nods out" while having a conversation, she isn't just tired: she's probably high. Although teenagers typically need a lot of sleep, there's a huge difference between the average teenager and one who's addicted to opioids. Many parents say that looking back, they realize they noticed signs that their teenager was using opioids, but did not understand them. Use your gut instincts here, and ask the parents of your teenager's friends whether they notice anything off about her.

WARNING BELLS: OPIOIDS
- Episodes of overwhelming fatigue
- Falling asleep at odd times
- Taking daylong naps
- Consistently missing school, work, or other activities to sleep
- Impaired thinking
- Inability to comprehend conversations
- Drooping eyelids
- Constricted (pinprick) pupils

The opioid-dependent teenager who stops using will suffer a very uncomfortable, but not physically dangerous, withdrawal that brings on anxiety, agitation, a runny nose, insomnia, muscle aches, and diarrhea. One term for withdrawal—"going cold turkey"—comes from the goosebumps that can appear during this process. The really bad part about withdrawal is that the excruciating ordeal often draws users back to the opioids. Your teenager knows exactly how to relieve the discomfort she's feeling: Get another opioid hit. If she makes it through the short-term withdrawal symptoms, longer-lasting insomnia might kick in. She might not sleep for two, three, or four nights in a row! Again, she knows exactly how to get some heavenly, immediate shut-eye. Withdrawal from the opioids makes relapse so tempting that decisive and quick treatment is essential. More on that later.

WHAT TO DO ABOUT OPIOID OVERDOSE

Teenagers often edge into using opioids, starting with the occasional prescription pill and then moving on to addictive use or injecting the drugs. Some teenagers can take opioids for a long time with little evidence of developing a tolerance to them. However, most teenagers who use opioids regularly become tolerant to their effects and feel less of a high from the usual dose. They need to take more and more opioids to achieve the same effect, so there's a built-in drive to take more drugs, try more potent drugs, or escalate to methods of snorting or injecting. Due to these effects, the risk of an overdose increases.

Opioid overdose can be lethal for your teenager. A true emergency, it can result in muscular paralysis, which causes him to stop breathing, or it can induce unconsciousness so deep that he cannot clear his throat should he vomit; in either case he will die of suffocation. If you can't arouse your teenager after he has taken opioids, you must act instantly! Call 911, then, if your teenager has stopped breathing and you can feel no pulse, initiate cardiopulmonary resuscitation (CPR). If he's breathing, turn him on his side so that if he vomits he won't choke on it. It's always a good idea to take an introductory course in first aid and CPR, but especially if your teenager uses opioids.

The best immediate treatment for opioid overdose is an under-the-skin injection or intranasal spritz of naltrexone (trade name Narcan®), a medication that immediately reverses the effects, waking up the victim and sending him into withdrawal right away.

Ambulances and hospital emergency rooms are usually stocked with this medication, and some programs for addicts actually hand out syringes prefilled with Narcan®. However, Narcan's® effects are very short-lived and anyone who has been revived by it requires on-the-spot attention from trained medical personnel. I hand out Narcan® kits to parents and family members of teens addicted to opioids, for use in the event that they find their child unconscious with a drug overdose. Do not hesitate to obtain a Narcan® kit from your local pharmacy, or a state-sponsored program, or your doctor's office. Contemplating using Narcan® is terrifying to parents. But it is a good idea to be prepared for the not-so-unlikely event of an overdose, and for all involved to acknowledge that the addictive use of opioids is indeed life threatening. Bottom line, there are no side effects for this medication, so even if you give a dose of Narcan® in the wrong situation, you won't be harming the person.

Opioid overdose can sometimes be blamed on a strategy used by drug dealers to gain an advantage over their competitors. They sometimes mix their product with other, more potent drugs, or poison, to boost its effects. News reports of overdoses and even deaths connected to a particular "brand" of heroin can set off a run on that brand, as users make the assumption that it's exceptionally potent.

Alongside overdosing is another danger posed by some prescription opioids. Drugs like Vicodin® are combinations of an opioid and acetaminophen (Tylenol®). This perfectly sensible pain-control formula becomes lethal when the drug is taken in large amounts. In the quest for a high, a teenager with a substantial opioid tolerance can unintentionally poison himself with the acetaminophen while attempting to take in enough of the opioid. Acetaminophen is toxic to the liver, so teenagers who use large amounts of these drugs can suffer severe liver damage.

SORTING OUT THE DIFFERENCES

All of the opioids target the opioid receptors in the brain and cause similar effects: pain relief, euphoria, sleepiness, muscle relaxation, and (sometimes) addiction, being the most prominent. The various opioids differ in how long they take to act, how long they stay in the body, and how they are ingested. For instance, methadone can be taken orally, takes effect in thirty minutes or so, and affects the user for four to six hours. By contrast, fentanyl (Duragesic®) is usually injected, works almost immediately, and lasts for only a few hours. (When used in a patch preparation, it can last longer.) These time frames are only estimates, because many of the opioids are used in ways other than intended. For instance, drug users can disable the timed-release mechanism of OxyContin®, snort the powder, and experience very intense effects.

Despite the differences among the more commonly abused opioids, they all have similar effects and your teenager can get addicted to any of them. In fact, the opioids are essentially interchangeable for teenagers: heroin can substitute for OxyContin®, which can substitute for Vicodin®.

Comparison of Commonly-Abused Opioids

Brand Name	Chemical Name	Ingestion Method	Length of Effect
Dilaudid®	Propoxyphene	Oral	4-6 hours
Dolophine®	Methadone	Oral	4-8 hours
Ms-Contin®	Morphine	Injection Oral	3-7 hours
N/A	Heroin	Snorted Injected	5-8 hours
OxyContin®	Oxycodone (controlled release)	Oral Snorted	3-6 hours
Vicodin®	Hydrocodone plus Acetaminophen	Oral	3-5 hours

WHY DO KIDS USE OPIOIDS?

A dose of opioids can produce euphoria, relaxation, and escape from pain, both physical and psychic. Although first-time users of heroin, whether they snort or inject it, often experience nausea, it lasts only briefly and is, for many users, more than compensated for by the pleasurable high. Addicted teenagers talk about gaining the ability to socialize with others, avoid difficult emotional issues, or even do mundane tasks like folding laundry. Of course, those who take too large of a dose become non-responsive or comatose, but new users who take the drug less often describe a blissful sense of transcendence and ease with the world.

However, the good part doesn't last forever. If your teenager becomes addicted to opioids, he needs to take the drugs just to feel normal. He may feel and look relatively unaffected when he's high, but quite obviously show the signs of withdrawal—sweats, dilated pupils, muscle cramps, diarrhea—when he isn't. This is one of the most chilling parts of opioid addiction: For your teenager, high becomes the new normal, and he needs the drug to function in ordinary life.

Tough Talk Dialog: "I Need It to Study."

Anne: *Son, I just can't believe you're on OxyContin. How long has it been going on for?*

Justin: *A few months—we were all trying it at a party...*

Bob: *A few months? You've seemed so, well, normal. You haven't looked high or anything. How can you be on OxyContin®?*

Justin: *It's not like that, Dad.*

Bob: *Not like what? Please explain this to me. It makes no sense.*

Justin: *Dad, I need it to study.*

Bob: *WHAT? Now you're seriously making no sense. How can you need to get high to study? You get straight As!*

Anne: *Calm down, Bob. We need to hear him out. What are you talking about?*

Justin: *That's just it. If I don't use the OxyContin® I feel terrible; I get the shivers, cramps, diarrhea, I can't sleep, and I definitely can't study. I take a few hits of the OxyContin® and I feel fine. That's when I can study.*

Bob: *I don't believe that.*

Justin: Well, it's true! That's why you can't tell that I'm using—I don't let myself get high. I just use every few hours.

Bob: That's hard to believe.

Anne: I think it's true. The school counselor said this had happened to two other boys in Justin's class.

Justin: There's medicine to help you get off. Dr. Wong can prescribe it, but you have to come with me.

Anne: Of course we'll come with you, honey. Right, Bob?

Bob: Yep. We're behind you in this, kiddo.

Anne and Bob are gravely concerned for their son's well-being and have armed themselves with the facts, so when Justin tells them he must use in order to study, they believe him. They're also prepared to get Justin the help he'll need to detox and get his life back.

TALKING TO YOUR OPIOID-USING TEENAGER

Discovering that your child is using or addicted to opioids can be a shocker. As parents, we react much more extremely to the idea of our teenager using heroin than if she's "just" using alcohol or marijuana. Despite your understandable shock and terror, it's possible to deal with the problem at hand.

Tough Talk Dialog: "HEROIN? How Could You?"

Arthur: Josie, your mom and I found more of those little plastic bags in the basement, and we found out what they are.

Josie: What, Dad? What are you talking about?

Betty: Those bags. That we found before with the powder residue in them. We asked Dr. Weiner what it is and he told us. It's heroin! How could you?

Josie: You're crazy, Mom. I have no idea...

Arthur: Enough, Josie. We called Andrea's mom and she said that Andrea is away at rehab for heroin, and that she has suspected for a while that you kids were doing it in the basement.

Josie: Well, OK. I might have tried it, but I just did it once.

Betty: *ARE YOU KIDDING ME? HEROIN?*

Arthur: *Josie, Mom and I are really upset about this, but we want to talk to you rationally. Dr. Weiner said that in his practice he's seen a lot of kids using heroin and even some who are addicted. He said we should find out how often you use it.*

Josie: *You're going to kill me if I tell you.*

Arthur: *We're worried sick about you, but we're going to talk to you reasonably about this and try to help.*

Josie: *Mom?*

Betty: *(Sobbing) We're going to try to help you.*

Arthur: *I'll be the designated talker here, OK? I'm just as worried as Mom, but I think I can get through this. How often have you been doing heroin?*

Josie: *Um... sometimes every day.*

Arthur: *How do you take it?*

Josie: *Dad! I just sniff it. I would never shoot anything!*

Arthur: *Good. That's one of the things he said to ask. Do you get withdrawals if you stop?*

Josie: *Well, I can't sleep, if that's what you mean—but I haven't tried to kick it in a while.*

Arthur: *OK. Dr. Weiner said he knows a place where you can get detoxed and back to yourself.*

Josie: *I don't need rehab! You guys are way too worried about this!*

Arthur: *Well, it's true we're freaked out. When we were kids, no one we knew used heroin.*

Josie: *Well, times have changed. We just use it to party.*

Arthur: *It sounds like you're stuck with it now, though.*

Josie: *I guess.*

Betty: *So, you'll go to the detox place?*

Josie: *I will if you two will just chill out. It's no big deal!*

Arthur: *We'll try, honey. We made an appointment for you this afternoon.*

Josie: *OK, but I still think you two are overreacting.*

Despite their alarm, Arthur and Betty stay resolutely on track to pushing Josie toward detox. They don't allow themselves to get drawn into a discussion of whether or not they're overreacting—they simply admit that they might be. Although they're glad that Josie doesn't inject the heroin, they don't let that deflect them from their purpose. While they know it's good she's not shooting up, it doesn't mean Josie doesn't have a problem with heroin.

USING OPIOID WITHDRAWAL TO GET YOUR TEENAGER INTO TREATMENT

Withdrawal from any opioid is uncomfortable and annoying, but usually not dangerous. It can involve intense craving, muscle aches, diarrhea, and impaired thinking, with insomnia that can last for weeks. You can use the torment of withdrawal to get your teenager into treatment, by assuring her that it's the quickest way to feel better. A detox center or a doctor specially licensed to prescribe a medication called buprenorphine can take the edge off your teenager's discomfort very quickly and then help her get treatment for her addiction. Offering the carrot of relief to get your teenager into treatment can be a highly effective strategy.

MAINTENANCE TREATMENT FOR OPIOID ADDICTION

Using an opioid medication like methadone or buprenorphine is called Medication Assisted Treatment (MAT): the addicted person is simply prescribed a similar medication, so he does not have to buy illegally, shoot up, or harm himself with adulterated street drugs. Although MAT is not necessarily the first method used for a person addicted to opioids, it does have its place within the armamentarium against opioid use. The maintenance opioid medications, when properly prescribed and monitored, can allow the addicted person to move on with his work, relationships, and physical well-being, in a way that is entirely consistent with good mental and physical health. This is because the maintenance medications are legal, administered orally, and take effect slowly. The effects last long enough so the person taking them does not become intoxicated, and if taken on a daily basis, will not experience withdrawal. I have seen teenagers whose lives have been saved by their use of maintenance medication. They can get off the merry-go-round of buying, using, and selling drugs for long enough to get their lives together. Although the person starting a maintenance program should intend to stay on the medication for at least a year or so, if and when he decides to taper off the medication, that tapering can be managed, so that it causes relatively little discomfort.

A common criticism of maintenance treatment is the following: "Maintenance treatment is just replacing one drug with another." My answer to that is that, yes, of course one drug is being replaced with another, but the drug that is now being used by the addicted teenager causes him no ill effects and allows him to move on with his life. Like all medications, the maintenance medications have benefits *and* risks. The downside of maintenance medication is that the addicted person then becomes physically dependent on the prescribed medication. However, when weighed against the soul-stealing power of the street opioids, maintenance medications look pretty good. Methadone must be prescribed by a federally licensed clinic or hospital, whereas buprenorphine can be prescribed in an office setting by a specially licensed physician. (Those physicians can be found at https://www.samhsa. gov/medication-assisted-treatment/physician-program-data/ treatment-physician-locator

BENZODIAZEPINES 101

Benzodiazepines are sedative medications prescribed for the treatment of anxiety, insomnia, alcohol withdrawal, and sometimes for muscle relaxation. Common examples are Valium®, Halcion®, and Xanax®. (Barbiturates such as Fioricet® and Fiorinal® are a different class of sedatives that can be lethal in combination with alcohol. They're less available to teenagers than benzodiazepines.) As occasional sedatives, these medications are in fact quite effective—to calm a patient during a brief dental procedure, say, or to alleviate a fear of flying, or to serve as a very short-term sleeping medication. Benzodiazepines are highly effective when used on an occasional basis, but they can be quite addictive. Just as worrisome, a person who abruptly stops taking benzodiazepines—most notoriously, alprazolam (Xanax®)—risks a withdrawal reaction that can include seizures.

When they were originally put on the market in 1960, the benzodiazepines were liberally prescribed, seen as relatively benign, and soon gained the nicknames "Mother's Little Helpers" and "Vitamin D" (for diazepam, brand name Valium®). However, it quickly became evident that those who take the benzodiazepines on a regular basis develop a tolerance and need higher and higher dosages to achieve the original sedative effects. It was also obvious that users frequently got addicted to these drugs; in fact, psychiatrists who prescribed them were once considered anathema for alcoholics. When they tried to cure alcoholism by prescribing Valium®, the inevitable result was addiction to the Valium®!

WARNING BELLS: BENZODIAZEPINES
- Lethargy
- Drooping eyelids
- Multiple trips to different doctors
- Bottles of pills in the house

HOW BENZODIAZEPINES AFFECT YOUR TEENAGER
So, what if your teenager's doctor says he "needs" a benzodiazepine? There are a few good reasons that a physician might prescribe a benzodiazepine for a teenager, most notably for the short-term treatment of alcohol withdrawal, or possibly to ease withdrawal from other drugs. Sometimes in these cases, benzodiazepines are absolutely necessary. While your teenager may be prescribed these medications for a legitimate purpose, if he takes them regularly, he'll get hooked on them. It's simple physiology. That's why today, doctors who treat withdrawal this way prescribe benzodiazepines very carefully and monitor their patients closely to avoid causing a new addiction.

It's almost never necessary, however, to use benzodiazepines to treat long-term symptoms, like anxiety or insomnia, in teenagers. Doctors usually put other strategies or nonaddictive medications into play when working with teenagers on these issues. If your teenager is prescribed a benzodiazepine, make sure his prescriber answers all of your questions about diagnosis, the overall treatment plan, and side effects.

Of course, if your teenager is "prescribing" her own benzodiazepines, you most certainly have a problem! Typically, teenagers who use benzodiazepines do so in addition to other drugs, or to self-treat withdrawal from alcohol or other drugs. Unfortunately, Xanax®—which causes vicious withdrawal and craving—is the most commonly abused of the bunch, because it takes effect very quickly. Since the cure for Xanax® craving or withdrawal is more Xanax®, teenagers sometimes find themselves taking very high doses, and they need to be detoxed very carefully to avoid seizures. It's relatively easy to buy or cadge small amounts of Xanax®, but large quantities are much more difficult to come by, therefore, teenagers sometimes find themselves unintentionally detoxing for the want of Xanax®.

Keep in mind that Xanax® is just one benzodiazepine, and these drugs aren't all the same. It's important to understand the similarities and differences between the various benzodiazepines that your teenager may have access to.

Comparison of Commonly Abused Benzodiazepines

Brand Name	Chemical Name	How Quickly Does it Enter the Brain?	How Long Does it Stay in the Body?
Ativan®	Lorazepam	Intermediate	10-20 hours
Halcion®	Triazolam	Rapid	1.5-5 hours
Klonopin®	Clonazepam	Intermediate	18-50 hours
Restoril®	Temazepam	Rapid	8-20 hours
Valium®	Diazepam	Rapid	30-100 hours
Xanax®	Alprazolam	Intermediate	6-20 hours

STEPS TO TAKE IF YOUR TEENAGER IS USING BENZODIAZEPINES

Don't be fooled by your teenager's claims that benzodiazepines are safe "because they're in all the pharmacies" or that "Julie's mom takes them every day." Just because they're legal and readily available doesn't mean these drugs aren't dangerous! Should your teenager become dependent, she'll manifest all of the typical signs of addiction, such as craving and needing more and more of the drug.

Benzodiazepine withdrawal can be uncomfortable and even dangerous: quitting suddenly can lead to seizures. Before your teenager stops using a benzodiazepine, first—and most importantly—get her a medical evaluation. A knowledgeable physician can design a detoxification schedule that will keep your child safe.

After addressing the physical upshots of benzodiazepine withdrawal, approach your teenager's addiction like any other. Make sure an addiction professional gives her a full evaluation and sets up the necessary detox help, relapse prevention therapy, and peer support, such as Alcoholics Anonymous. Your benzodiazepine-addicted teenager needs treatment, and treatment works!

POINTS TO REMEMBER

- Immediately call 911 if your teenager overdoses on opioids!
- Don't be surprised if your teenager seems normal when high on opioids, or uses them to study.
- Use the promise of relief from the misery of opioid withdrawal as the "carrot" to get your teenager to treatment.
- Make sure your benzodiazepine-using teenager has a medical evaluation before stopping use.

Chapter 7

PERFORMANCE-ENHANCING DRUGS: PRESCRIPTION STIMULANTS AND STEROIDS

If ten kill you, I'll take nine.
—Tom Simpson, late English Elite Cyclist

Teenagers use performance-enhancing drugs (PEDs), including substances that might not seem to be performance enhancers, for many reasons. PEDs improve academic, physical, and athletic ability, allowing teenagers to function at higher-than-normal levels. Teenagers misuse all sorts of substances to improve their proficiency at various tasks. The most common examples are prescription stimulants like methylphenidate and amphetamine, the active ingredients in widely used attention deficit disorder (ADD) medications, which help students focus on schoolwork and get better grades. Meanwhile, teenagers who play sports will sometimes use anabolic steroids to boost their muscle mass, strength, and speed. Even more teenagers use anabolic steroids to bulk up for cosmetic reasons. Be warned that although steroids don't usually cause classic addiction, stimulants most certainly do.

Marked improvement in your teenager's athletic or academic improvement isn't necessarily suspect—for most kids, it's simply the result of hard work. However, in some cases, coaches, teachers, and parents want so much for their young athletes and students to succeed that they miss PED clues that are evident to others.

Ask the obvious questions if you notice anything out of the ordinary about your teenager's progress: If she's suddenly getting better grades, ask her what she's doing differently. If he's suddenly become a star on the field, ask him how he's done it. Also, keep an eye out for changes in your teenager's behavior and appearance.

FOCUSED AND ENERGETIC: THE TEMPTATIONS OF STIMULANT MEDICATIONS

There are many performance-enhancing stimulants; most readily available to teenagers today are methylphenidate and amphetamine, the active ingredients in, among others, the commonly prescribed attention deficit disorder (ADD) medications Ritalin® and Adderall®, respectively. The majority of prescription stimulants come in the form of pills, and some also come in transdermal patches. These FDA-approved stimulants are most often used for perfectly legitimate purposes, such as the treatment of depression, but for teenagers, it is usually for the treatment of ADD.

Even if your teenager's doctor prescribes stimulants for him, they can become a problem. Teenagers have learned that these medications, intended to improve a person's emotional health and overall well-being, can be misused, especially to help them study. They obtain the drugs on the sly from friends or dealers, or they simply abuse the stimulants that their doctor prescribes. Teenagers can crush the pills and snort the powder to get a very quick and effective high.

The unmonitored or improper use of stimulant medications can produce serious side effects and can be a disaster. When they are used compulsively or addictively, they cause more harm than good. In my office I see teenagers who can't sleep because they snort Ritalin® and Adderall®, or who go into withdrawal if they stop the drugs. If your teenager has been prescribed a stimulant, it's up to you to keep track of how many pills he's taking. Whether or not he's supposed to be taking stimulants, watch out for their side effects and other unwanted impacts, such as loss of appetite, sleep problems, or unstable moods. Such actions can signal misuse. If you see these, hand over your teenager's treatment to an experienced addiction clinician!

THE LONG AND SHORT OF STIMULANT MEDICATIONS

If a knowledgeable clinician determines that your teenager needs a stimulant medication for Attention Deficit Disorder, then selects a medication carefully, closely monitors its use, and conducts regular follow-ups, this type of drug can have a life-altering positive impact with few or no side effects. Beyond a doubt, prescription stimulants can be enormously beneficial for teenagers suffering from ADD or depression, and they're often the treatment of choice (but they aren't the only treatment option).

Different stimulant medications have different effects, and teenagers are more likely to abuse or become addicted to certain ones. Pharmaceutical companies engineer drugs like Ritalin® (methylphenidate) and Adderall® (amphetamine/dextroamphetamine) in different preparations that take effect in and act for varying lengths of time. The prescription stimulants fit into short-acting and long-acting categories. The short-acting medications, such as Adderall Immediate Release (IR)®, give a quick "bump" in mood and enhance the ability to concentrate, which many teenagers experience as pleasurable. Those who are prescribed this sort of stimulant sometimes find these more effective than the long-acting options, but kids are also most likely to abuse and to become addicted to them. Long-acting medications such as Adderall Extended Release (XR)® last all day and are less addictive than their short-acting counterparts, but some teenagers find they are not as effective. Neither long-acting nor short-acting medication is better or worse. One or the other might not be right for every patient: They are just different.

Short-Acting Stimulant Medications

Brand Name	Generic Name	Commonly Prescribed for	Starting Dose	Maximum Dose	Length of Action
Adderall®	Mixed amphetamine salts	ADD	2.5 mgs	60 mgs	4 hours
Dexedrine®	Amphetamine	ADD, obesity, narcolepsy	2.5 mgs	40 mgs	4 hours
Focalin®	Dexmethylphenidate hydrochloride	ADD, narcolepsy	5 mgs	60 mgs	4 hours
Ritalin®	Methylphenidate hydrochloride	ADD, substance dependence, narcolepsy	5 mgs	60 mgs	4 hours

Long-Acting Stimulant Medications

Brand Name	Generic Name	Commonly Prescribed for	Starting Dose	Maximum Dose	Length of Action
Daytrana™	Methylphenidate patch	ADD	10 mgs	30 mgs	12 hours
Ritalin SR®	Methylphenidate hydrochloride, sustained release	ADD, narcolepsy	10 mgs	60 mgs	Up to 8 hours
Vyvanse®	Lisdexamfetamine dimesylate	ADD	30 mgs	70 mgs	10 hours

IS MY TEENAGER MISUSING STIMULANT MEDICATION?

If your teenager is taking stimulant medication without close medical supervision, she's at the very least, not getting its full benefits, and at worst, may be doing serious damage to herself. A teenager who takes too much of her own medication, uses someone else's pills, or crushes and snorts stimulant pills is endangering herself and needs treatment. Like a cocaine addict, she might be losing weight, struggling with insomnia, plagued with agitation or having tremors. Nonetheless, her grades may be going up. PEDs are so diverse that the warning bells for abuse vary.

WARNING BELLS: STIMULANT MEDICATIONS

- Rapid and unexplained improvement in academic performance
- Abrupt weight loss
- Insomnia or ability to stay up all night
- Agitation

WHAT ABOUT ADD MEDICATIONS AND ADDICTION?

Prescription stimulants such as Adderall® and Ritalin® have some effects similar to those of illicit stimulants such as cocaine. This can be very confusing to kids and parents alike, who know how much these medications can help teenagers live up to their full potential, both academically and socially. Despite their benefits, the drugs can trigger some of addiction's hallmark symptoms: compulsive use, drug-related health problems, and ongoing consumption despite the harm caused. The potential and actual side effects of stimulant medications can certainly be devastating, but ADD sufferers who are carefully diagnosed, prescribed, and monitored are unlikely to become addicted. In fact, research shows that stimulants like Adderall® and Ritalin®, when taken as prescribed, actually protect addiction-vulnerable teens against developing addictions!

Since doctors prescribe stimulant medications to so many teenagers, high school and college campuses are often flooded with huge supplies available for the selling or stealing. Many students see stimulants as valuable study tools and don't think there's anything wrong with breaking some rules to improve their grades.

Tough Talk Dialog: "Everyone Uses Ritalin® to Study!"

William: *Sis, I cannot believe you stole your roommate's Ritalin® and snorted it. How could you do that?*

Heather: *Oh, please. Everyone uses Ritalin® to study. It's how you get through college and into law school, and I certainly need it.*

William: *Not everyone.*

Heather: *Like you didn't? Seriously? You're that smart?*

William: *No, I'm not, but I do know that I got through college and into law school without it. The problem with using those drugs to study is that you need to take more and more, and eventually you have to snort them just to get up. Law school is tough, so you've got to take them, then comes the bar exam. And after that, you're practicing law, which is pretty damn hard. You going to use that stuff your whole life?*

Heather: *Maybe I should. Maybe I have ADD.*

William: *Maybe you do, but you should get checked out for it and get some legit help.*

Heather: *I am getting some help for it. I'm helping myself!*

William: *You're not doing a great job of it. Stealing things and jamming them up your nose doesn't help.*

Like Heather, some users who use un-prescribed stimulants may be self-medicating their undiagnosed ADD. Most of these kids don't benefit long-term because the drug or dosage is ill-matched to their needs and the side effects go unmanaged. When someone takes another person's medication without proper diagnosis or monitoring, all bets are off!

A lot of teenagers take stimulant medication just to get high, either by overdosing on pills or by snorting it in powdered form.

The negative effects of these medications, when they're used contrary to medical advice, can be just as disastrous as those of street drugs like cocaine. Again, the legality of a substance, or the legitimacy of a prescription, matter less than how your teenager is using it. Don't get hung up on anything other than the well-being of your teenager.

GOOD MEDICINE GONE BAD

Obviously, there's a big difference between the appropriate use of stimulant medications and the inappropriate use of the very same substances. It doesn't matter if a doctor prescribes the medication, because teenagers often abuse their prescription drugs in harmful ways. The number one reason that teenagers abuse stimulants is to enhance their performance in school, a goal that their parents usually share. Of course, most parents would not want their teenager to endanger himself in the pursuit of a good GPA, which is exactly what happens when a teenager uses stimulants haphazardly and without careful medical supervision.

Many high school and college kids share, exchange, sell, and buy stimulant medications among themselves as illicit study aids; they can even get the drugs off the Internet. Teenagers with untreated ADD can easily—and illegally—obtain stimulant medications in order to self-medicate their very real psychiatric disorder. If your teenager has been prescribed stimulant medication for any reason, don't hesitate to ask if he ever shares his medication with friends or if it has ever been lost or stolen. If your teenager doesn't have a prescription, ask if his friends ever share theirs with him. These are signs of trouble and need to be addressed immediately.

Tough Talk Dialog: "I Just Use It for Tests."
Chris: *Mom, Dad, I know you guys are mad about those pills, but you shouldn't have been looking in my backpack anyway!*
Albert: *Maybe so, but where did you get them?*

Chris:	*That's personal! Mom, look what he's doing! It's none of his business.*
Mom:	*Dad and I talked about this and we're on the same page, Chris. We need to know what's going on here, since this could be dangerous for you.*
Chris:	*Oh, please. Dangerous? I'm doing exactly what you want me to do. My grades are always better when I take the pills before tests, and I just use them for tests.*
Albert:	*We never told you to take drugs!*
Mom:	*OK, OK, let's all take it easy for a second here. We're less concerned about where you got them and more concerned about what happens when you use them. So tell us, what happens?*
Chris:	*What happens? I do better on my tests, that's what happens.*
Albert:	*Your mom's right. We're on your side, Chris. What else happens?*
Chris:	*Nothing. I study better.*
Mom:	*It's your appetite too, sweetheart. Maybe that's why you've been losing weight.*
Chris:	*Well, I want to lose weight. It's a good thing!*
Mom:	*Maybe, maybe not. Now that I think about it, you've been staying up so late all month—maybe that's because of the pills.*
Chris:	*Well, maybe.*
Albert:	*Do you grind the pills up and snort them?*
Chris:	*DAD! I'm not a drug addict! I would never do that!*
Mom:	*No one's accusing you. We just want to help you the best we can.*
Chris:	*You're not mad?*
Albert:	*We're mad, but we're more than that, we're worried about you. Mom and I talked about this after we found the pills—we can get you an appointment so you can deal with what you're doing, and find out if you have ADD or some other learning problem.*

Chris: *I do have it.*

Mom: *Could be. If you do this the right way you can get some help for whatever holds you back in school, without all this drama. Maybe it's not ADD. Whatever it is, you can get help for it, rather than just taking your friend's pills. We don't want you to hurt yourself just to get good grades.*

Chris: *Neither do I, really.*

Albert and Andrea acknowledge that they are in fact angry about Chris's drug use, but they focus on their more pressing concern, his well-being. Importantly, they acknowledge that Chris may be self-medicating a real problem, but advocate getting an evaluation, rather than just assuming that it's ADD.

STRONG AND SEXY: THE ALLURE OF ANABOLIC STEROIDS

Anabolic steroids do one thing for the body: they increase the amount of circulating testosterone, which, when combined with exercise, enhances physical performance by enlarging muscles and (in some people) increasing muscle strength. Teenagers take them not to get high, but to succeed in sports or to get buff. Anabolic steroid use doesn't necessarily cause physical dependence, but is a serious cause for parental concern.

Anabolic steroids are popularly known as steroids or 'roids. Due to a number of famous athletes having been caught using these illegal performance-enhancing substances, the drugs have had a heavy news presence over the last several years. Oftentimes, teenagers use them to improve athletic performance, and find that the drugs make a big difference, despite the fact that using anabolic steroids this way is illegal and considered cheating by all legitimate sports organizations.

Using anabolic steroids might start out as an easy route to remarkable weight-lifting results, achievement in gym class, and success in extracurricular sports, but the drugs often become a purely cosmetic tool. Some teenagers take anabolic steroids to build larger muscles in order to look more attractive and grab some sexual attention from their peers. Although girls as well as boys do this, high school males are the most frequent users. In the same way that some teenage girls—and boys—contract eating disorders, starving themselves into skinny and unhealthy abnormalities, some boys—and girls—build themselves up into muscular behemoths.

KNOW YOUR ANABOLIC STEROIDS

Technically known as anabolic androgenic steroids, or AAS, the muscle-building steroids, such as Nandrolone® and Stanazolol®, are derivatives of testosterone. Testosterone itself is sometimes prescribed for legitimate reasons, as are anabolic steroids, to help treat serious medical conditions such as muscle wasting syndromes, AIDS, and testicular dysfunction. They should not be confused with corticosteroids, which aren't addictive and are legitimately used for the treatment of asthma, joint inflammation, and dermatitis.

Steroids can be taken orally or by injection and can remain in the body for periods from a few hours up to many months. With increasing public knowledge of the dangers of steroids, users face increased scrutiny, but an underground industry has sprung up to provide steroids, pseudo-steroids, and steroid-boosting supplements. Some of the supplements are legal, safe, and possibly effective, but others are clearly illegal and sold under the radar. Any supplement that's claimed to increase testosterone or build muscles quickly is suspect. If you have questions about a particular supplement or brand of supplement, you can check websites like the FDA's consumer education site (https://www.fda.gov/food/dietarysupplements/usingdietarysupplements/) for information as well as for suggestions on finding out about a particular substance.

Commonly-Abused Anabolic Steroids

Trade Name	Generic Name	How it's Taken	Detection Time on Testing
Depo-Testosterone®	Testosterone Cypionate	Injected into muscle	3 months
Deca-Duroblin®	Nandralone Decanoate	Injected into muscle	18 months
Equipoise®	Boldenone	Injected into muscle	5 months
Winstrol®	Stanazolol	Oral	3 weeks
Dianabol®	Methandrostenelone	Oral	6 weeks
Oxandrin®	Oxandrolone	Oral	3 weeks

RECOGNIZING STEROID USE

Since your teenager isn't typically drug tested for steroids unless he participates in organized sports, you'll have to learn to recognize steroid use without the benefit of lab work. Use your instincts. If your teenager suddenly sprouts muscles out of proportion to his body size, ask if he's taking steroids. Gym teachers and coaches may be the first to recognize this sort of change in your teenager's body, so keep in close touch with them if you start seeing changes. Steroids have other effects that you should also look out for and ask your teenager about. Frustratingly, some signs of steroid use mimic the normal changes in your teenager's body.

WARNING BELLS: STEROIDS

- Rapid muscle growth
- Sudden increase in weight
- Significant improvement in athletic performance
- Facial acne
- Emotional instability
- Testicular shrinkage (in boys)
- Growth of facial hair (in girls)
- Growth of breast tissue (in boys)

If you notice any of these symptoms in your teenager, ask him if he's using, check out the local gym, and talk to his coaches about it. You may find that steroid use is very common among your teenager's friends and teammates. When you try to convince him that he needs help, you may run into some resistance from your teenager, who might see no harm in illegally using a pharmaceutical to improve his performance or physique. It's vital that you keep at it and not become easily deterred by his aggression.

Tough Talk Dialog: "The Pros Do It!"

James: *Son, I see that you're really bulking up this summer.*

Jerry: *Getting ready for football, Dad. I'm all set to go!*

James: *Well, yeah, but are you using anything to help you?*

Jerry: *Sure. I work out at the gym every day and go heavy on the protein shakes.*

James: *It looks to me like you've been going heavy on something else—I checked out those bottles in your closet and a lot of them are steroids!*

Jerry: *You spied on me? You came into my room?*

James: *I did, because I'm worried about you and it looks like I have something to be worried about!*

Jerry: *You don't. Those are all protein powders. I just mix them up and have them in the morning before I work out.*

James: *Come on, Jerry, those aren't protein powders. I know what Diannabol® is. I played football too.*

Jerry: *Well, maybe I tried it. I needed it to get big for the line next season! All the pros do it!*

James: *Never mind that. It's not safe.*

Jerry: *Oh, please. You want me to make the team, don't you?*

James: *I do, but not at the expense of your health. I've never wanted that!*

Jerry: *Well, I really don't want to get sick, but I do want to make the team. The guys at the gym tell me what to do so I don't have any problems.*

James: *Well, you've got a problem now. I won't let you do it. I made an appointment for this afternoon with a doctor who Dr. Schwartz says can get you off this stuff.*

Jerry: *It's really none of your business, Dad. I'm going to be seventeen in two months, you know!*

James: *It's my business. I love you and I'm worried for you.*

When you speak with your steroid-using teenager, merely state that you're worried—steroids are dangerous—and move on to getting him some help. A long discussion about steroids' dangers and potential dangers, or about the ethical issues surrounding performance enhancement, would be off the mark. Focus on your teenager's illegal and dangerous drug use and on getting him the help he needs.

THE DOWNSIDES OF STEROIDS

For teenage athletes, the steroid strategy can unfortunately backfire, because steroids can have unintended effects. Users might find that steroids' effects actually end up undermining their performance; for instance, their massive muscles can impede agility. Vanity bodybuilders also face pitfalls: Their distorted body image points toward future problems with physical health and emotional development.

High school athletes risk dangers as well. In recent years, it's become increasingly likely that they will be tested for drugs. Although high school drug testing programs are in their infancy, they're becoming more and more sophisticated and soon enough teenagers who use steroids will have nowhere to hide. A teenage athlete who gets caught using drugs will be banned from her sport, putting an end not only to her high school ambitions, but to any dreams of a college scholarship or professional athletic career. Even if she squeaks by in high school, she can be certain she'll be caught by the very accurate and comprehensive drug screenings conducted by the NCAA and professional sports leagues. She has almost no chance of achieving her ultimate goal.

No matter why your teenager takes steroids, they can have detrimental health consequences. Using steroids before reaching full physical maturity can prematurely stop bone growth. There are also sexual side effects, which are particularly disturbing to young men, who often have no idea what might occur. Excess testosterone in your son's system is converted to female hormones, causing breast growth and testicle shrinkage. Steroids can also shut down his normal testosterone production, so that when your teenager quits steroids his testosterone levels drop and he can no longer achieve an erection. Meanwhile, women who use steroids or testosterone over the long term can find it difficult or impossible to conceive a child.

Most alarming, though, is what can happen if your teenager abruptly stops using steroids, especially if she's been using them in high doses. Suddenly depriving the body of these drugs can cause uncomfortable and sometimes dangerous withdrawal. Teenagers often take steroids in massive overdoses, risking an emotional crash into depression, insomnia, and even suicidal thinking and behavior if they withdraw. If you suspect that your teenager is a steroid user, don't insist that he stop immediately. Instead, insist that he let an experienced addiction clinician help him quit!

Too often, parents who discover that their teenager is using steroids demand that he stop then and there, unaware that untreated steroid withdrawal can result in suicidal behavior. One tragic example is a young athlete named Taylor Hooton, who died in 2004. A seventeen-year-old from Plano, Texas, he went off steroids abruptly and committed suicide soon afterward. It's too simplistic to say that steroid use or withdrawal directly causes suicide, but the drugs clearly make teenagers vulnerable to emotional turmoil and self-destructive behavior. Be prepared if you find out your child is using steroids, and get knowledgeable professional help immediately!

TREATING STEROID USE: A TEAM APPROACH

Since your steroid-using teenager must be weaned off the drugs safely, he should be treated by a team that includes an endocrinologist (a specialist in hormone diseases) and a mental health clinician, both of whom are knowledgeable about the medical problems faced by steroid users. After an initial evaluation, which usually involves blood tests and an MRI scan of the brain, your teenager's endocrinologist will recommend a course of treatment designed to return the child's hormonal system to its normal function. The treatment sometimes includes adding hormone supplements, and sometimes consists of withdrawing all medications to see how your teenager's endocrine system responds. Both strategies can result in depression, or at least mood instability, so it's absolutely necessary that a mental health clinician regularly monitor the process. As a parent, you should insist from the beginning that the treatment team remains in close contact with one another and that any changes you observe are quickly heard and addressed.

POINTS TO REMEMBER

- Professionally evaluate attention deficit disorder (ADD), don't just treat it.
- Teenagers can easily—and illegally—obtain commonly prescribed stimulant medications, such as Ritalin® and Adderall®.
- Weight loss and insomnia suggest stimulant use.
- Sudden muscle growth suggests steroid use.
- Abruptly quitting steroids can lead to depression, insomnia, and suicidal thinking and behavior.
- An endocrinologist and mental health clinician should supervise steroid withdrawal.

Chapter 8

ADDICTIONS TO SEX, FOOD, AND GAMBLING

A student undergoing a word-association test was asked why a snowstorm put him in mind of sex. He replied frankly: "Because everything does."
— Honor Tracy, twentieth-century English author

Addictions to sex, food, and gambling (and even shopping) are often called "behavioral" or "spectrum" addictions, because they aren't only about getting high, but about getting too much of a good thing. Basic human behavior like eating, sexuality, or taking chances are all normal and necessary for survival, but when routine behavior becomes compulsive and destructive, it certainly looks like addiction. In fact, psychiatric assessment of people who behave compulsively around food, sex, and gambling reveals patterns of thinking and action that are remarkably similar to those of alcoholics and drug addicts.

Sometimes people joke about or trivialize these sorts of compulsive behaviors, but playing them down reflects a profound misunderstanding of the human pain involved. It's deadly serious when a teenage girl binges and purges, or when a teenage boy obsessively watches Internet pornography instead of connecting with friends, schoolwork, or sports. The common thread in behavioral addictions is compulsive, self-destructive behavior.

Clinicians who treat behavioral addictions often say that they are different from addictions to drugs or alcohol because you can't lock the tiger in a cage and throw away the key. With food, you have to take the tiger out for a walk three times a day. With sex, the tiger also has to come out and play. Even with gambling, the tiger has a role to play: living life means taking risks. You can certainly try a zero-tolerance policy for drugs, alcohol, sex, or gambling for your teenager, but you can't really institute a policy like that for eating, or even for dieting.

HOW TO RECOGNIZE PROBLEMS WITH FOOD, SEX, AND GAMBLING

If your teenager's relationship to food, sex, or gambling is compulsive or self-destructive, you probably wonder, "Isn't confusion normal at this age?" Teenage experimentation is indeed a fundamental part of growing up, by which we discover our limits and figure out how we want to live our lives. As with drugs or alcohol, trying out risky activities can morph into intensely self-harming and pathological behavior that can have a permanent—and ruinous—impact on your teenager's life. The definition of compulsive behavior is often subjective, but when it comes to your child, the judgment is yours to make.

Don't wait until your teenager's behavior becomes unavoidably destructive before you take action. Rather, intervene early and often to help him manage his behavior and to get some help from a specialist. If you have questions about your teenager's eating, sexual, or gambling behavior, don't keep them to yourself. Ask friends, family members, and mental health clinicians for their take on the situation. It's a good way to separate parental worry about normal teenage risk taking from worry about more serious and potentially injurious behavior.

WARNING BELLS: FOOD, SEX, AND GAMBLING ADDICTIONS

- Doing "too much" eating, dieting, sexual behavior, or gambling
- Focusing on food, sex, or gambling to the exclusion of friends, schoolwork, or extracurricular activities

RECOGNIZING YOUR TEENAGER'S EATING DISORDER

Eating disorders are very common among teenagers, especially girls. The most common eating disorders are anorexia nervosa (extreme weight control via self-starvation and/or excessive exercise) and bulimia (vomiting—"purging"—after binging on food). They stem in part from the pressures teenagers feel in the face of cultural ideals of beauty; peer, parental, and teacher messages about desirable body size; and the body's natural tendency toward a certain weight. No wonder the teenage psyche is crammed with all sorts of distressing body-image issues.

Eating disorders share many traits with other addictions. They, too, are compulsive, self-destructive and difficult to overcome, and have serious health consequences. In fact, teenagers with eating disorders have high mortality rates and must be treated quickly and aggressively.

Teenagers—mostly, but not always, girls—who suffer from anorexia have a distorted body image that leads them to restrict the number of calories they take in, often to the point of dangerous weight loss. Similarly, teenagers with bulimia go through binge-and-purge cycles in which they gorge themselves with carbohydrates then make themselves vomit, or use laxatives to rid themselves of the unwanted calories.

In addition, eating disorders are often associated with addiction to substances: many anorexics use cocaine and other stimulants to suppress their appetite and attain a very low weight. If you see the symptoms of an eating disorder in your teenager, seek professional help.

WARNING BELLS: EATING

- Continual talking about food and weight
- Severe or rapid weight loss
- Extreme dieting or exercise
- Food or meal avoidance
- Binging or evidence of binging (large quantities of food gone, wrappers in the trash, etc.)
- Purging (often spending an inordinate amount of time in the bathroom after a meal)

FACING YOUR TEENAGER'S EATING DISORDER

Just like abusers of drugs and alcohol, teenagers with eating disorders may persist in mind-blowing denial. "How can you not see that you're starving yourself?" many a parent has wanted to scream at their anorexic daughter—but screaming has little effect. Don't take her denial personally; instead, focus on the disorder itself.

Tough Talk Dialog: "I Just Want To Be in Shape."

Ms. Singh: *Katy, could I talk to you a minute?*

Katy: *Sure, Ms. S., what's up?*

Ms. Singh: *Katy, I've been meaning to mention that in gym class I can't help but notice that you've lost a lot of weight lately.*

Katy: *Yeah, isn't it cool? I'm really getting in shape!*

Ms. Singh: *To tell the truth, I'm not so sure you're losing it in a healthy way. You've lost maybe twenty pounds since the summer, and that was only three months ago!*

Katy: *Yeah, I've really been trying, and it's paid off. What's the big deal?*

Ms. Singh: *Well, I know it's not healthy to lose weight that quickly and frankly, you look scrawny rather than fit—your workouts are way too intense!*

Katy: *What? You're the gym teacher, and you always tell us to push ourselves. I just want to be in shape.*

Ms. Singh: *I've never told any of you kids to go off the deep end, and it looks to me like that's what you're doing. You're getting weak instead of strong.*

Katy: *I'm not doing anything weird, though!*

Ms. Singh: *Mrs. Cranston in the library told me that you look at those "pro-ana" websites about how to be anorexic.*

Katy: *So, you guys are spying on me? Who cares what websites I go to?*

Ms. Singh: *We're just worried about you. I care about you and don't want you to get sick!*

Katy: *I'm not sick. I'm trying to get thin and look good.*
               Anyway, you're *skinny.*
Ms. Singh: *Not like you. I try to eat healthy every day and not let*
               my weight drop too low.
Katy: *What, are you a doctor now?*
Ms. Singh: *(Laughs) Nope, but Ms. Morales, the guidance coun-*
               selor, said she would be happy to see you and that
               she worries about you, too. She can refer you to an
               anorexia doctor.
Katy: *You guys are worried about nothing. I feel great.*
Ms. Singh: *Maybe so, but will you go along with me and see the*
               guidance counselor?
Katy: *There's nothing wrong with me, but OK, I'll go.*
Ms. Singh: *That's great, Katy. You can use my phone right now to*
               make an appointment.

Ms. Singh doesn't get into a discussion about how thin is too thin, she merely states her observations. Katy has lost a lot of weight quickly, appears gaunt, and is surfing websites that endorse anorexia. Ms. Singh wisely refers Katy to the guidance counselor, who can initiate treatment and knows the available community resources.

GETTING TREATMENT FOR YOUR TEENAGER'S EATING DISORDER

If you see that your teenager is losing weight rapidly or if she looks too skinny, immediately have her examined by a pediatrician. This is nonnegotiable. Anorexia and bulimia can kill, so you should react the same way you would if your teenager was shooting cocaine—or stepping in front of a bus.

Skilled practitioners use a substantial store of knowledge in treating anorexics and bulimics. The treatment can be complicated and often requires a commitment of many years. (Long-term treatment is beyond our scope here; some good books and websites are listed in the Readers' Resources section of the appendix.) Sometimes treatment must start with a relatively short inpatient hospitalization designed to bring your teenager back to a healthy weight and launch a course of psychotherapy.

Psychotherapy for eating disorders is typically cognitive-behavioral in style, focused on the here and now and on recognizing the disordered thoughts involved in anorexia and bulimia, and some medications are helpful. Oftentimes family members will be included to support healthy eating behavior, discourage unhealthy ones, and watch out for potential disasters. Your teenager's therapy can help you get a handle on your reactions to her problematic thinking and eating habits. It can also teach you skills for helping her modify her unrealistic thoughts and dangerous eating habits.

Your teenager might receive a dual diagnosis of an eating disorder plus substance abuse. Both conditions should be treated at the same time. Some parents wonder whether their daughter uses cocaine or other stimulants to stay thin or if her low weight is just an outcome of substance abuse. At the beginning of treatment, when your daughter's health is the most urgent issue, trying to sort this out is a waste of time: She must focus on beating both the drugs and the eating disorder. When those are under control, she can explore the connection between them.

UNDERSTANDING TEENAGE SEXUALITY

Although research shows a downward trend in teenage sexual behavior over the last ten years, a 2016 report published by the federal government reveals that a significant number of teenagers are sexually active. A report by the Centers for Disease Control and Prevention, published in *Morbidity and Mortality Weekly Report,* stated that in 2015, 41 percent of high school students reported that they had had sexual intercourse, and 3.9 percent said that they had had sexual intercourse before the age of 13. Of sexually active teenagers, 56.9 percent had used a condom during their most recent sexual intercourse, and 20.6 percent had used alcohol and/or drugs before that encounter.

Most teenage sexual behavior isn't worrisome, but you naturally respond to your teenager's sexuality based on your own experiences, values, and preconceptions. As a parent you have the right to set the parameters for your teenager's sexual behavior, whether abstinence before marriage, insistence on meeting his friends, or requiring the use of condoms. Know, however, that you're no more likely to control your teenager's sexual behavior than any other parents have been throughout history.

If your teenager deviates from your standards, it doesn't indicate that he has sexual problems. Likewise, your teenager's age when he first experiments or has intercourse is unrelated to sexual addiction. Nor does sexual addiction have anything to do with your teenager's sexual orientation or even his number of partners. Sexual addiction isn't, in fact, about having a high sex drive, any more than alcoholism is about having an unquenchable thirst.

HOW DO I KNOW IT'S SEXUAL ADDICTION?

The best definition of sexual addiction that I've seen comes from sex addiction therapist Patrick Carnes on www.sexhelp.com. He defines sexual addiction as "...any sexually-related, compulsive behavior which interferes with normal living and causes severe stress on family, friends, loved ones, and one's work environment." For teenagers, the interference with "normal living" is the essential piece. Whether we call it sexual addiction, sexual compulsivity, or love addiction, sexuality that takes over your teenager's life interferes with normal living. An obsessive desire for new and different sexual partners and experiences can dominate your teenager's life and can damage his health, immediately or in the long term.

What does sexual addiction look like? Sexual addiction clinicians have identified a number of problem areas for teenagers, but what matters for you is your teenager's behavior. A promiscuous teenager might try to bolster his self-esteem by making multiple sexual conquests, but find each one unsatisfying and thus seek out more sex. A teenager who discovers cocaine and sex at the same time and can't disentangle the two might develop unhealthy attachments to drug dealers and users; these might become her paradigm for loving relationships. (In fact, sexually addictive behavior is often mixed up with drugs and alcohol.) Extreme examples, yes, but they illustrate the uncanny power of sexuality to derail a young life. This kind of sexual behavior is dangerous and might signal that your teenager has become addicted to sex.

WARNING BELLS: SEX
- Multiple sexual partners; promiscuity
- Sexting: sending sexually explicit pictures or texts to others
- Posting sexual images on social media sites
- Drug- or alcohol-fueled sexual behavior
- Exhibitionism
- Having sex in exchange for money, drugs, or other compensation

TALKING TO YOUR TEENAGER ABOUT SEXUAL ADDICTION
If your teenager engages in questionable sexual behavior, he likely needs help. It's difficult to have any conversation about sex with your teenager, especially if you believe, correctly or not, that he's sexually addicted or has another sexual problem. Yet, if he's a sex addict, it's your job to address the problem just as if he was hurting himself with alcohol or cocaine.

First, put the issues on the table as matter-of-factly as possible—which I realize is a nearly impossible task. Couch your concerns in terms of what's healthy for your teenager, rather than in terms of your own values, your concept of what's normal, or what you want for your child. After bringing the subject up, ask if there are other issues you should know about: drug or alcohol use, payment for sexual favors, sexual abuse, and encounters with sexual predators (either other teenagers or adults). Once you determine (as best you can) what your teenager is doing and whether it's connected to other addictive behavior, you'll have to make some choices. Do you believe what your child's telling you? In the light of day, does his sexual behavior appear harmless and age appropriate? If so, you might choose to back off or ask more questions.

Tough Talk Dialog: "My Sex Life is None of Your Business!"

Robert: My Internet is down!

Alice: Yes, it is, son. Dad and I put a password on the router so you can't use it for now.

Robert: What for? I need to be able to go online!

Alex: Mom and I really feel that we need to shut it off. Like we told you last week, we're concerned about all that time you spend looking at porn sites.

Robert: I told you! Everyone looks at those sometimes—it's normal. I just surf by to see what's going on.

Alice: Oh come on, honey. We looked at your credit card bill last month—you spent $300 on those sites and chatting and whatever else.

Robert: I'll pay you back. That was just a mistake last month—I didn't know how much they were going to charge me.

Alex: It's not just the money. You're actually flunking two classes—you've gotten all the way to twelfth grade and never flunked a class or even gotten below a B.

Robert: I'm just under a lot of pressure.

Alex: Come on, son, we know you spend all your time in your room online, looking at girls. It's pretty logical for us to think that's the problem, right? Unless you're doing drugs, but it doesn't look like you are.

Robert: I'm not! So what if I like to look at girls on the Internet. I'm a teenage boy, you know!

Alex: I know—I was a teenage boy myself, but you've dropped all your friends and your other activities. It looks to me like you've cut yourself off from real girls, and real people for that matter!

Robert: My sex life is none of your business. You said you would never bug me about that.

Alice: It's not your sex life we're worried about—it's the rest of your life. You're failing classes, you've dropped your friends and are spending enormous amounts of money for sex stuff on the Internet. We're worried about you.

Alex:	We arranged for you to see Dr. Schneider, a therapist who deals with this, tomorrow after school.
Robert:	Oh please, I'm not going to talk to anyone else about this. He'll just tell you all my private stuff. It's none of his business! Besides, you guys are just old-school—you have no idea what goes on now! You just want me to be like you, and I'm not!
Alice:	No, Dr. Schneider already told me and Dad that he won't pass on anything you say unless it's life threatening. We agreed to that.
Robert:	So you've been talking about me behind my back?
Alex:	It's only because we're worried about you. We don't want to intrude, but we obviously have to in this circumstance.
Robert:	Right. When can I get back online?
Alice:	As soon as you and Dr. Schneider decide it's safe. We all need some help in dealing with this.
Robert:	What? I have to see this guy in order to use the Internet?
Alex:	We don't want to set things up for you to fail at this, son. We'll be open to turning your connection back on and unlocking the credit card when you're safe.
Robert:	You're totally pressuring me with this!
Alice:	I guess we are, son.

Alice and Alex stay focused on their concern for their son's emotional and financial well-being, as well as his growing isolation from his peers. They're not drawn into discussions about their son's privacy or their own sexual values.

HELPING YOUR SEX-ADDICTED TEENAGER

Urgent: If it seems to you that your teenager is involved in unsafe or exploitive sexual behavior, you must act immediately! Call the police if a crime has been committed. You're obligated to protect your child and others from dangers such as sexual predators. Reacting immediately and decisively also sends the message that you absolutely forbid certain behavior under any circumstance.

Most likely, however, your teenager won't have gone so far. A professional therapist who's knowledgeable about sexual addiction will need to assess the addictive sexual behavior, along with any other addiction issues. When it comes to sexual addiction, perhaps even more so than with drug or alcohol addiction, the therapist must give your teenager a solid assurance of confidentiality. The therapy will be doomed if the therapist is—or is perceived as—a conduit to you.

Should your teenager need inpatient treatment, her therapist can provide access to appropriate treatment facilities, most of which are segregated by gender. Her therapist might also prescribe certain medications, generally a serotonin-specific uptake inhibitor (SSRI) such as Prozac® or Zoloft®. In high doses, these medications reduce compulsive behavior of all sorts, including sexual compulsivity. In addition, peer-led support groups can benefit your teenager. Groups like Sexual Compulsives Anonymous (SCA) can be tremendously helpful for adults, but ask your child's therapist whether any local groups are appropriate for teenagers.

HOW MUCH GAMBLING IS TOO MUCH?

Although teenagers—and adults—often romanticize gambling, people who gamble too much can run into serious financial, emotional, and relationship problems. Gambling is legal for adults in more and more venues, but there's a very good reason that minors are restricted from almost every kind of gambling. Teenagers typically lack the judgment, self-awareness, and caution they need to safely wager small amounts of money and walk away from a loss. (Of course, many adults also lack these capabilities!)

Nevertheless, teenagers now have many opportunities to go wild with gambling: Not only can they do the usual betting with friends or on poker nights, they can gamble with electronic arcade or video games, at online casinos, through organized sports betting, and as underage gamers in bricks-and-mortar casinos. For the teenager with a propensity to gamble, the wide variety of easily accessible gambling opportunities can lead to disaster, especially when he combines gambling with drugs or alcohol. The majority of problem gamblers are male.

As with the other behavioral addictions, a gambling problem or addiction can be recognized by the harm it causes the gambler. The most obvious damage is financial, but gambling also can—and often does—result in ruined relationships with family or friends, trouble with schoolwork, or legal problems. A 2000 report in the *Journal of Gambling Studies* neatly itemized some of the more problematic behavior and attitudes of teenagers with gambling problems.

WARNING BELLS: GAMBLING
- Preoccupation with gambling
- Gambling online or at high stakes
- Chasing losses with more bets
- Lying to family or friends about gambling
- Using lunch money or allowance to gamble
- Requests for unreasonable amounts of money
- Missing school to gamble
- Stealing from family to gamble

TALKING TO YOUR GAMBLING-ADDICTED TEENAGER
When you bring up gambling with your teenager, he will of course deny, at least initially, that he has a problem. You'll probably have to listen to blather about teenagers having fun, the hoary old excuse that "everyone does it," and even the argument that gambling is a harmless way to earn a little spending money. Don't question your own perception of the problem and don't wait too long to intervene. If your teenager's gambling is spinning out of control, broach the subject gently but forthrightly, and express your worries. When he tries to derail the discussion by arguing, stay focused on his gambling.

Tough Talk Dialog: "Don't You Want Me To Make My Own Money?"

Bonnie: Sammy, I want to talk to you about your gambling.

Sammy: OK Mom, but we've already had this discussion.

Bonnie: I know, kiddo, but I'm getting more worried about it and I talked to Billy's dad about the poker parties you guys have. He says you sit around and drink beer and you've lost your shirt the last few weeks.

Sammy: What? You've been spying on me?

Bonnie: I'm allowed to—you're only sixteen. The point is that other parents are worried also and you guys are betting with money you don't have. It worries me and I think it should worry you.

Sammy: (Shouting) YOU SPIED ON ME! I TOLD YOU NOT TO!

Bonnie: OK, Sammy, I know it upsets you, but sometimes I need to do it. Your gambling is getting out of control. Where do you get the money for it?

Sammy: Geez, Mom. I get it from my allowance and what I saved from my summer job.

Bonnie: That's not possible, son. I understand that you lost $220 last week, you don't have that much.

Sammy: Oh please, Mom. Everyone takes a little chance once in a while. Dad does it! He goes to Vegas all the time. Don't you want me to make my own money?

Bonnie: Not by gambling and we're not talking about Dad. It's you I'm worried about. I'm going to have to hold back on your allowance and not allow you to go to poker night any more.

Sammy: What? That's so embarrassing. The guys will laugh their heads off at me! Anyway, you can't stop me—I'll just go online to gamble.

Bonnie: Well, I know you've tried that also—and I might have to shut down the wireless network in the house.

Sammy: *That's crazy! I can always find a way to gamble if I want! I need to do it! It calms me down.*

Bonnie: *Yeah, that's what I thought. I've got some ideas for helping with that. There's a therapist downtown who specializes in gambling and there's even a group he recommended that you can try out this weekend. You can go to that instead of your poker night.*

Sammy: *Are you kidding me?*

Bonnie: *Nope.*

Bonnie was able to stay on track despite Sammy's attempts to deny the problem, but your teenager may present more challenges. Gamblers Anonymous has developed a helpful set of twenty questions (www.gamblersanonymous.org/20questions.html) to identify gambling problems: Put them to your teenager and see if he says "yes" to any of them. It might help you—and him—to acknowledge his gambling addiction. Most compulsive gamblers will answer yes to at least seven of these questions.

TWENTY QUESTIONS FROM GAMBLERS ANONYMOUS

- Did you ever lose time from work or school due to gambling?
- Has gambling ever made your home life unhappy?
- Did gambling affect your reputation?
- Have you ever felt remorse after gambling?
- Did you ever gamble to get money with which to pay debts or otherwise solve financial difficulties?
- Did gambling cause a decrease in your ambition or efficiency?
- After losing, did you feel you must return as soon as possible and win back your losses?
- After a win, did you have a strong urge to return and win more?
- Did you often gamble until your last dollar was gone?
- Did you ever borrow to finance your gambling?

- Have you ever sold anything to finance gambling?
- Were you reluctant to use "gambling money" for normal expenditures?
- Did gambling make you careless of the welfare of yourself or your family?
- Did you ever gamble longer than you had planned?
- Have you ever gambled to escape worry, trouble, boredom, or loneliness?
- Have you ever committed, or considered committing, an illegal act to finance gambling?
- Did gambling cause you to have difficulty in sleeping?
- Do arguments, disappointments, or frustrations create within you an urge to gamble?
- Did you ever have an urge to celebrate any good fortune by a few hours of gambling?
- Have you ever considered self-destruction or suicide as a result of your gambling?

HOW TO HANDLE YOUR TEENAGER'S GAMBLING

There are a few concrete steps that you can take if you find out that your teenager is gambling compulsively. First, limit the funds that you provide to him and restrict gambling opportunities that you have allowed him, such as Internet access. Second, take your teenager to a therapist who has experience working with teenage problem gamblers. The therapist should be an addiction professional who's dealt with other compulsive disorders, since gambling problems rarely appear alone. Your teenager may need help with various addictions, depression, or other psychiatric conditions.

Third, encourage your teenager to get involved in Gamblers Anonymous (www.gamblersanonymous.org), a group that functions along the same lines as Alcoholics Anonymous. It provides peer support and practical techniques, and encourages gamblers to acknowledge that even a little bit of gambling can lead to trouble. The "out-of-control" aspect of compulsive gambling is very similar to that of substance abuse, which is why 12-step groups are so helpful.

Finally, remain vigilant for the return of any gambling behavior. Teenagers have ample opportunities to gamble, so enlist the help of a professional therapist to monitor your teenager's finances, whereabouts, and attitudes.

POINTS TO REMEMBER

- Listen to your gut. If your teenager's compulsive behavior worries you, you're probably right.
- Get feedback from others about your concerns.
- Obsessions with food, sex, or gambling are danger signals for behavioral addiction.
- When confronted, your teenager will likely deny having an eating, sexual, or gambling problem.
- Compulsive and damaging behavior requires professional treatment.

Chapter 9

DUAL DIAGNOSIS: MENTAL ILLNESS AND ADDICTION

I may be a drug addict, but I'm not crazy!
—Ed, Patient, Bellevue Hospital, New York City

When I served as Unit Chief of the Dual Diagnosis Unit at Bellevue Hospital in New York City, I learned a lot about how to treat addictions combined with mental illness, and about how to guide families in helping their mentally ill addicted teenagers. There's a lot you can do for your teenager in this situation if you know how to work within, manage, and even manipulate the health-care system that's treating her.

A teenager who suffers from both addiction and mental illness has a condition termed "dual diagnosis." For example, a physician would give a dual diagnosis to a teenager who is addicted to alcohol and has major depression. In concert with each other, the conditions that comprise your teenager's dual diagnosis can cause serious damage. Although upsetting to all involved, a dual diagnosis isn't the end of the world.

With the sophisticated treatment available today, your teenager can get her addiction and her mental illness treated at the same time. If she stops or reduces her intake of problem substances while getting good psychiatric treatment, she can experience rapid and long-lasting improvement. Having spent most of my career treating dually diagnosed people, I can attest to the amazing recovery attained by many.

RECOGNIZING MENTAL ILLNESS

A discussion of the many different forms of mental illness is beyond the scope of this book (I recommend a few good references in the Readers' Resources list in the appendices). It's important, however, for you to recognize the red flags that can indicate your teenager is suffering from a psychological disorder of some kind. Although each syndrome has its own set of symptoms, you should be most concerned about serious signals that call for immediate professional evaluation and about more acute signs that indicate your teenager's life might be in danger.

WARNING BELLS: MENTAL ILLNESS

Acute: Call 911 Immediately!
- Suicidal thoughts
- Hints about suicide
- Homicidal thoughts or hints

Serious: Get an Evaluation Immediately!
- Hallucinations (seeing or hearing things that aren't there)
- Delusions (fixed, false, and often paranoid beliefs)
- Over-suspiciousness
- Severe isolation
- Odd beliefs
- Extreme religiosity

If your teenager is homicidal or suicidal you MUST call 911 NOW. The "serious" warning bells alert you to get help for your teenager right away. Don't write off troubling behavior as an effect of drug use or "just a phase." Take it seriously.

Tough Talk Dialog: "He's Just Going Through a Phase."

Arlene: Honey, you're making too big a deal about this. We just need to give Bobby his privacy. He's a teenager, you know!

Bill: I do know, but I'm bothered by him staying in his room and smoking pot all the time. He's totally cut himself off from school and his friends.

Arlene: He's just going through a phase—all teenagers do that. Anyway, he's finding new friends.

Bill: He's not seeing anyone, though. What about those things he said about the police last night?

Arlene: That they were chasing him with ray guns? He was kidding! Couldn't you tell?

Bill: He didn't look like he was kidding. He looked scared out of his mind.

Arlene: Maybe it's all that pot.

Bill: Could be, but we have to get him to a doctor, no matter what he says. This is too scary.

Arlene: I guess you're right.

It's far beyond your ability—or mine—to tell if someone who talks about suicide will make a serious attempt on his life or if he's instead trying to express that he's in deep distress. In any case, the distinction is unimportant. I've seen teenagers who clearly don't intend to take their own life make a desperate maneuver and accidentally kill themselves in the process. Don't try to guess what's going on with your suicidal, hallucinating, or delusional teenager. You must get help immediately.

MAKING A DUAL DIAGNOSIS

Of course, the symptoms of mental illness and addiction often mimic each other and are tricky to sort out. The vast majority of psychiatric symptoms can be caused by both mental illness and substance problems, making it difficult to determine a clear diagnosis. There are a few symptoms that occur in the case of addiction alone, but the exact same symptoms can occur when only mental illness is present—and those symptoms can also mean that your teenager is suffering both from addiction and mental illness. Confused? You're not alone.

Substance use, whether illicit or legal, always makes the evaluation and treatment of mental illness more complicated. Only a knowledgeable clinician who's familiar with both mental illness and addiction can properly evaluate your teenager. Usually this is a psychiatrist or a psychologist, although sometimes an experienced social worker or addiction counselor can make a diagnosis.

Teenagers with psychic distress—like depression or anxiety—may "self-medicate" themselves by using substances to relieve their pain. It's not hard to understand why a socially anxious young woman might drink alcohol in order to socialize more comfortably with others, nor is it hard to understand how that strategy might end up in disaster. Similarly, a depressed young person might use cocaine in order to perk himself up for school, or work, or just interactions with other people. Of course, many substances of abuse can cause the exact symptoms they are used to "treat." Often enough, the teen's apparent self-medication is just part of a self-reinforcing cycle of pain, drug and alcohol use, and more pain.

Symptoms of Addiction, Mental Illness, and Dual Diagnosis

Addiction Only	Mental Illness Only	Dual Diagnosis: Addiction Plus Mental Illness
– Craving	– Sadness	– Sadness
– Withdrawal	– Anxiety	– Anxiety
– Tolerance	– Insomnia	– Insomnia
	– Agitation	– Agitation
	– Lack of appetite	– Lack of appetite
	– Hallucinations	– Hallucinations
	– Delusions	– Delusions
	– Solitariness	– Solitariness
	– Suicidal thoughts	– Suicidal thoughts
	– Disorganized thinking	– Disorganized thinking
		– Craving
		– Withdrawal
		– Tolerance

DO DRUGS AND ALCOHOL CAUSE MENTAL ILLNESS?

The interplay between drugs, alcohol, and mental illness differs from one syndrome to the next. Parents often ask me about four conditions in particular.

Depression

Think of depression as a symptom, like fever, and you'll quickly understand that depression has many different causes. Just as strep throat or a virus or a toe infection can cause fever, drugs or alcohol can also likewise cause depression, or depression can come from a congenital chemical imbalance, or by painful life events. Alcohol and drug use can worsen depression; nevertheless, depressed teenagers often try to treat their sadness and demoralization with those substances.

Whichever comes first—the depression or the substance use—it's quite clear that the substance use must stop before psychiatric treatment can be successful. Throwing vodka on a smoldering problem can cause a bonfire.

Anxiety

As with depression, anxiety can cause, result from, and be intensified by substance use. There are legitimate medications that treat anxiety related to alcohol and illicit drugs, but it's possible to become addicted to some of them. This addiction can cause further anxiety. Here's how it works: A short-acting sedative medication, such as Xanax® (alprazolam), works perfectly well to calm down someone who's nervous, anxious, or afraid. For instance, even if she's afraid of flying, she can board an airplane and even catch a few winks as it takes off, but within a few hours her medication wears off, causing "rebound anxiety." She feels worse than she did before she took the medication. A perfect cure for this feeling is more medication, but there's never enough to stop this cycle of ups and downs.

Don't get me wrong: Properly prescribed sedatives don't always cause these sorts of effects, because many people can ignore the rebound anxiety and take the medication only occasionally and as directed. However, those who are susceptible to addiction—including teenagers with a dual diagnosis—should avoid sedatives. Only if absolutely necessary should a doctor prescribe them, and then, only with the utmost caution.

Bipolar Disorder

Bipolar disorder, typically an alternating pattern of very high/irritable moods (mania) and very low moods (depression), is often associated with drugs and alcohol, in part because bipolar teenagers have obviously impaired judgment that can mimic the effects of intoxication. Illicit drugs, especially stimulants like cocaine and alcohol often worsen bipolar disorder, though symptoms caused only by the substances don't constitute bipolar disorder. For instance, cocaine makes most users giddy and energetic, as if they are in a manic state, but their mood wears off when the cocaine does.

Due to the grandiosity associated with mania and the hopelessness that often accompanies depression, many bipolar teenagers find it difficult to give up drugs and alcohol—but it can be done. In my own practice, I've seen many bipolar teenagers with a dual diagnosis learn to manage their symptoms by avoiding drugs and alcohol, in the same way that a diabetic can control his illness by avoiding sugar. "I just can't go there" is their mantra.

SCHIZOPHRENIA

A serious mental illness that usually emerges between the ages of sixteen and twenty-five, schizophrenia causes odd behavior, a severe tendency to isolate from others, and a loss of contact with reality. Drugs and alcohol can't cause the disease, but they can certainly produce symptoms that mimic those of schizophrenia, or perhaps cause it to appear at an earlier age. Don't assume that your teenager's frightening symptoms, such as hallucinations or delusions, are "just" an effect of substance use. Don't just hope they'll go away on their own. While I recommend that you keep from overreacting in many other situations related to substance use, when hallucinations or delusions appear you must respond assertively. If your teenager is having "psychotic" symptoms—a break with reality—it's vital to get immediate professional help to keep him safe, identify the underlying causes, and get him the treatment he needs.

STARTING TREATMENT

As with a teenager who is "only" using substances, the first priority is to keep your dually diagnosed teenager out of harm's way, as best you can. At the beginning, you probably won't be able to tell how much of your child's behavior is due to mental illness and how much is due to drugs or alcohol. Don't worry. The best psychiatrist in the world can't figure that out right away. What we psychiatrists can do is keep an open mind about the diagnosis while keeping the patient safe, flushing drugs and alcohol out of her body and—this is important—treating both her addiction and her mental illness at the same time. Your teenager shouldn't have to wait around for all of the substances to clear out of her system before she can get evaluated and treated for depression, nor should she have to wait to get addiction treatment until her treatment for depression is underway. The best treatment systems offer integrated, simultaneous treatment of both conditions.

In order to have your teenager evaluated, you'll need to find a knowledgeable clinician—a psychiatrist or psychologist, or maybe an experienced social worker or addiction counselor—who has a solid track record treating both mental illness and addiction. Any large hospital's psychiatric department is certain to include clinicians who are trained in handling the challenges of dual diagnosis. Chapter 10: "How to Find Good Treatment and Get Your Teenager to It" has more information on how to search for a competent clinician. Ask about the clinician's training and experience with both mental illness and addiction, and make sure you're satisfied before you choose one to treat your teenager. After you find a clinician, you'll need to get your teenager to the clinician's office or facility, which is sometimes an even more difficult task than if addiction is the only issue. If your teenager is profoundly depressed or anxious, just leaving the house may seem like an insurmountable task, but as with addiction, you can use your leverage as a parent to convince, cajole, or even mandate that she see the therapist. If these tactics don't work, your assurance that treatment offers relief from the unbearable feelings caused by mental illness as well as addiction will most likely persuade your teenager to give therapy a try.

MAKING THE SYSTEM WORK FOR YOU

For reasons that I can't cover here, our society generally takes mental illness more seriously than addiction, both legally and financially. Rarely do the authorities require addicts to have an evaluation, but many laws and regulations allow the involuntary hospitalization of certain mentally ill people. Our society does stigmatize mental illness, but health insurance plans are more likely to pay for its treatment than for addiction therapy.

On the financial front, hospitals and other treatment facilities know that health insurance plans usually shell out more readily for the treatment of mental illness than of addiction. When you seek out help for your teenager, work with his health-care providers to find the dual diagnosis that will best help you pay for the therapy he needs. Absolutely don't misrepresent his illness; just highlight the aspects that will ensure reimbursement so your teenager will be treated. You've either paid your private insurer the premiums that entitle your child to psychiatric treatment, or your publicly provided Medicaid or Children's Health Insurance Program (CHIP) covers it. Make sure your teenager reaps the benefits of health insurance!

When it comes to the law, teenagers who suffer from bipolar disorder, schizophrenia, or suicidal depression may be legally coerced—physically if necessary—to submit to psychiatric evaluation. In some cases, law enforcement officers have the authority to compel hospitalization, but they're usually reluctant to do this. You're probably horrified that your child can be restrained and taken to the hospital against his will, but sometimes it's the only way to save his life. If your teenager's addiction and/or mental illness are so dire that you need to get the legal system involved, the mental illness factor can actually work to your advantage. Focusing officials' attention on your teenager's psychiatric symptoms rather than on his addictive behavior can increase the likelihood that he'll get treatment.

For instance, if your teenager has isolated himself to the point that he's barricaded himself in his room, emphasizing his depression is more likely to convince the authorities to intervene and possibly mandate treatment, even if you suspect marijuana is at the root of his behavior. Explain the problem to the powers-that-be in the way that will be most helpful to your teenager. Sure, gaming the system may seem manipulative, but this sort of strategy might be the only effective weapon you have in your battle against your child's combined addiction and mental illness.

MEDICATING YOUR TEENAGER'S DUAL DIAGNOSIS

A wide variety of medications are used to treat the dual diagnosis of addiction plus mental illness. For instance, the mood stabilizing medications like lithium and Depakote® can also treat the impulsivity that often leads to substance use, and antidepressant medications like Prozac® and Zoloft® can (sometimes) alleviate the crushing depression that can lead teens to use drugs. However, these—and all—psychiatric medications have very limited effects if the teenager is still using drugs and alcohol. This is the central conundrum of treating the dually diagnosed teenager, and the reason that the treatment of addiction and psychiatric illness must be simultaneous.

Some of the medications, such as Ativan®, Ritalin®, and Suboxone®, that doctors prescribe to dually diagnosed teenagers are potentially addictive. Along with the good such medications can do for a teenager with a dual diagnosis, is the risk of causing or worsening his addiction problem. While it might be a good idea to prescribe a week or two worth of, say, Ativan®, for an anxious teenager who's not an addict, the drug might cause a new addiction in a teenager who does suffer from addiction. Certainly, these kinds of drugs can be helpful, but only a psychiatrist who is knowledgeable about addiction and who closely watches for signs of addictive behavior should prescribe these medications. In this situation—the treatment of a teenager who has both a psychiatric illness and an addiction issue—there is no substitute for an addiction psychiatrist.

As a parent, you need to know about the medications that your teenager's doctor might prescribe, and come to your own judgments about them. Ask yourself a simple question: do the benefits (or potential benefits) outweigh the risks (or potential risks) of this medication for my dually diagnosed child? Learn about the drug's effects and side effects through conversations with your teenager's psychiatrist, advice from other well-versed psychiatrists, and reading the medical literature.

If you turn to the Internet for information, take what you read with a grain of salt. Separate the hype of advertisers and exaggerations of anti-medication zealots from reality. I recommend that you trust only government- and university-based websites, and well-known medical information sites like WebMD. Discuss what you find on the Internet with your teenager's physician to make sure that you're getting good, accurate information relevant to your teenager's specific dual diagnosis. Above all, use your common sense.

Your teenager might reject the medication prescribed for him on the basis that substances caused his problems in the first place. He might wonder why he should take a chance with another substance. Support his healthy skepticism about substances, but address his concerns and offer knowledgeable reassurance.

Tough Talk Dialog: "I Just Don't Like the Idea of Taking Medications."

Bill: *Are you kidding me, Mom? They want me to take another drug and you agree with them?*

Anna: *Well, yes, I do. The doctor went over all the benefits of taking it and told me the potential risks. It makes sense to me.*

Bill: *That's crazy—drugs got me acting all freaky in the first place. Why would I take another one, just because some doctor says it's safe?*

Anna: *That's a great attitude—I really mean it. I'm glad you're becoming aware of what you put into your body, and I guess it's fair to look at all substances the same way. Like the doctor said, cocaine, sugar, and cyanide are all white powders, but they have different effects. You're smart to think about that.*

Bill: *I guess so. I just don't like the idea of taking medications.*

Anna: *Me either, but I think this one is worth it for you. If it helps with those mood swings, it will certainly be worth it!*

Anna acknowledges and, in part, supports her son's skeptical attitude about medication, but makes the point that an appropriately prescribed medication is different than a street drug. She stays focused on helping her son, rather than entering into a philosophical debate about substances, societal views, prescribing practice, etc.

IS MY TEENAGER BEING OVERMEDICATED?

Dually diagnosed teenagers can easily be overmedicated with psychiatric drugs. Occasionally, they're improperly overmedicated to control unruly or disruptive behavior, but more often than not, your teenager's prescribing physician is overprescribing in an attempt to quell dangerous or disturbing symptoms. Unfortunately, the effects of hidden drug and alcohol use can mimic psychiatric symptoms and lead physicians to prescribe medications to treat those symptoms, when a better strategy would be to simply rid the teenager of her substance of abuse. For instance, a teenager with cocaine-induced manic episodes followed by crashing depressions could easily be misdiagnosed as having bipolar disorder, and treated with the appropriate medications for that condition. To avoid this, your teenager's prescribing doctor should first do a complete diagnostic assessment, then continually evaluate dosages and side effects, and take care not to prescribe unnecessary medications.

Your teenager's psychiatrist should include you and your dually diagnosed child in any decisions regarding medication. Only through collaborative effort can you determine the best possible regimen with the best effects and the fewest side effects. To prevent overmedication, make sure that you know the target symptoms each medication is supposed to treat. For example, one target symptom for aspirin is *headache*. Target symptoms for Prozac®, meanwhile, include *hopelessness* and *isolation*. By focusing on target symptoms, you can see whether a medication is having the desired effects or is being prescribed repeatedly and thoughtlessly, without consideration of changing the dosage or prescribing other medications that might be more effective.

IS MY TEENAGER BEING UNDERMEDICATED?

Just as worrisome as overmedicating a dually diagnosed teenager, is undermedicating. Out of a misguided fear of psychiatric drugs, your teenager's physician might sometimes hold back needed medications. Sometimes, families insist on too low a dosage—or no medication at all. Although all medications have risks, and some medications present the risk of addiction, always weigh those factors against the benefits that a particular drug might have for your teenager. Think of psychiatric medication the same way you think about medications for other illnesses: Some chemotherapy medications have serious side effects and risks, yet can cure cancer.

If your teenager has ongoing psychiatric symptoms after giving up substances, perhaps she's being undermedicated. For instance, if she stopped using cocaine several months ago, but still suffers from mood problems, sleeplessness, or poor appetite, she may need psychiatric medication. If the clinician you're working with doesn't agree, get a second opinion.

STOPPING PSYCHIATRIC MEDICATIONS

At some point, your dually diagnosed teenager might decide that he no longer needs or wants medication. Be aware that poorly considered changes in medication—and certainly changes that aren't recommended or monitored by a psychiatrist—can have disastrous effects, including seizures, mood swings, and suicidal thoughts. Abruptly stopping certain psychiatric medications can cause withdrawal and, over the long term, the resurgence of symptoms that the medication was treating. For example, a seventeen-year-old girl whom I was treating followed her older sister's advice to stop taking the antidepressant Zoloft®. When she did, she suffered several days' worth of irritability and sleeplessness, until those symptoms gave way to the general anxiety that the Zoloft® had treated quite satisfactorily. Your teenager must stop psychiatric medication only with the assistance of the prescribing physician!

Typical Effects of Abruptly Stopping Some Psychiatric Medications

Class of Medication	Names of Medications	Effects of Stopping Abruptly	Comments
Benzodiazepines	Ativan® (lorazepam) Halcion® (triazolam) Restoril® (temazepam) Valium® (diazepam) Xanax® (alprazolam)	Seizure, tremors, mood instability	Xanax® and Halcion® are the two benzodiazepines most likely to have withdrawal effects.
SSRI antidepressants	Celexa® (citalopram) Paxil® (paroxetine) Prozac® (fluoxetine) Zoloft® (sertraline)	Anxiety, insomnia, irritability	Paxil® is notorious for causing withdrawal effects.
Opioids	Methadone® (dolophine) Suboxone®/Subutex® (buprenorphine)	Insomnia, chills, sweats, muscle cramps, tearing eyes, running nose	Side effects are almost guaranteed with the abrupt elimination of any opioid medication.

POINTS TO REMEMBER

- Drug or alcohol use and mental illness can have similar symptoms.
- Call 911 immediately if your teenager is having suicidal thoughts, hallucinations, or delusions.
- Mental illness can cause, result from, and be intensified by substance use.
- Focusing on the mental illness component of your teenager's dual diagnosis can help you find and fund good treatment.
- Know the target symptoms for and side effects of any medication prescribed for your dually diagnosed teenager.

SECTION III:

THE BEST POSSIBLE TREATMENT

Chapter 10

HOW TO FIND GOOD TREATMENT AND GET YOUR TEENAGER TO IT

Our greatest glory is not in never failing, but in rising up every time we fail.

—Ralph Waldo Emerson

In her iconic song, "Rehab," English soul singer Amy Winehouse said that she refused to go to addiction rehab because she "ain't got the time." Sadly though, by the time her substance use became problematic and evident to those around her, Winehouse couldn't quit without help. She died in 2011 at the age of twenty-seven, a month after "she stumbled onto the stage in Belgrade and gave an incoherent performance appearing very disorientated and removed from reality," the *UK Daily Mail* reported.

DOES MY TEENAGER NEED HELP?

You can be sure that by the time you notice your teenager's difficulties, she's probably in crisis. Like adult substance users, teenagers who use substances can be quite adept at hiding their use and its effects. It's a rule of thumb that when your teenager tells you how much she's using, she's actually using quadruple that amount.

Bottom line, if you know she has a problem, it's time to get her into treatment.

Gauging the severity of your teenager's substance problem may be particularly confusing if she lies when you ask about it. Lying is always part of addiction, as is denial, the psychological blockade that prevents many addicts from acknowledging the seriousness of their problem. Regardless of why or to what extent your teenager is misleading you, the task at hand is to cut through the misinformation as best you can. At the least, try to outline the extent of her problem, and decide on treatment based on that outline.

This is where an addiction clinician—an expert in helping people with addiction—can be of immense assistance. He or she can help you assess the immediate risks to your teenager, ferret out problems that you may not have even considered, and put together an appropriate treatment plan. No clinician is a human lie detector, and none can know exactly the depth of your teenager's difficulties, but a well-trained therapist has both the experience and the emotional distance to formulate a solid treatment plan.

SHOULD I TEST MY TEENAGER FOR DRUGS AND ALCOHOL?

Home drug and alcohol tests of various sorts are widely available in drugstores and online, but they serve little purpose unless you handle them without a glitch and you put the results to good use. Urine tests, breathalyzers, and substance-testing kits are also available at your local drugstore, but I don't recommend that you use them. In my view—whether your substance-using teenager has never been treated, is currently in treatment, or has left treatment—his drug and alcohol testing should be performed by professionals, rather than by you.

Although I've seen some families use home drug and alcohol testing to effectively help their teenager, it rarely works out that way. Home testing conducted by parents more often adds fuel to the substance-use fire because parents usually mishandle and misinterpret them, and subsequently misuse positive results to punish their teenager rather than to get him into treatment. I've heard too many stories of pointless family screaming matches that start with a home-testing kit. Taking the do-it-yourself route can easily worsen your relationship with your teenager. Don't take that risk.

It's not that any drug testing is perfect, but drug testing interpreted by a laboratory or experienced clinician is a lot more likely to be accurate, and the clinician interpreting the test can then use the results to modify the treatment. Even if done properly and read correctly, home testing can't tell you when, or for how long, your teenager has been using substances. Although teenagers can—and often do—manipulate drug tests, there are some innocent explanations for positive results, such as ingestion of harmless substances or over-dilution from an expected source. Even a negative test can be misleading, since intentional urine dilution can cause a false-negative, and tests do not necessarily include the relevant substances: only some opioids are included in most of the available over-the-counter urine tests, for instance. An addiction professional knows what to look for. And, the teenager's emotional response to the testing process, the results, or the consequences of those results can be used in the treatment. It's much more helpful to your teenager—and to you—for you to be a loving (if self-limiting) parent, rather than a substance-use monitor. Let the professionals be the bad guys if need be!

I'm not saying that you shouldn't have your teenager tested if you're suspicious, just that you should have it done correctly. When you decide that the time has come, ask a qualified addiction clinician to perform or arrange for a professional test, and to follow up afterward. (If your teenager does not yet have a personal clinician and you've gotten to the point of drug testing, he probably needs one.) Unlike you, a clinician can look at your teenager's situation dispassionately. She'll obtain better results and will be able to use them in a nonpunitive way to get your teenager the help he needs. Whoever tests your teenager, the issue of trust is always at the forefront.

Tough Talk Dialog: "You Don't Trust Me!"

Leah: Mom, I can't believe you want me to pee in a cup just so you can test me. It's so embarrassing! Why would I agree to go to outpatient treatment if I wasn't going to stop using cocaine?

Elena: Well, the program tests the people who go there, and it sounds like a good idea to us.

Leah: Really? Dad?

Ken: Sure. They know what they're doing at the clinic, so I guess I agree with drug testing.

Leah: I can't believe you two! You don't trust me! After everything I've done, and now I'm going to outpatient and you still don't trust me! That's crazy.

Ken: Like the counselor said at orientation, that's part of addiction. We just can't rely on you to tell the truth about your use.

Leah: Oh, that's a cop-out, Dad. You just don't trust me.

Elena: You've given us plenty of reason NOT to trust you over the past several months, at least about drugs and alcohol.

Leah: Oh my God! I can't believe you're not giving me credit for the three weeks I've been clean. I've done everything you've said. It's so not fair!

Ken: We certainly do give you credit for the past three weeks, which have been great, but like your counselor said, addiction isn't that easy to beat. We're looking for some support to help you stay clean. It'll take some time to regain our trust completely, but you're certainly on the way.

Ken reasonably gives Leah the credit she deserves—the last three weeks have been great—but he doesn't trust that three good weeks mean she's beaten her addiction. This attitude of hopeful skepticism is a difficult, but honest position to take. It's also realistic and a good model for the addicted teenager.

CHOOSING A THERAPIST

To refer to addiction therapists of every kind I've intentionally used the broad term "clinician" since it's more important that the person who helps your teenager deal with his substance problem knows a lot about addiction treatment, rather than having a certain credential. Some addiction counselors are superb in this role, as are social workers, psychologists, and psychiatrists. Academic or medical credentials rarely tell you what you need to know about a clinician's training and experience regarding addiction. Don't hesitate to ask for a curriculum vitae (résumé) or a brief rundown of the clinician's experience. If you were looking for someone to work on your car, you would certainly make sure that they had some experience with your make and model!

Many people who are "in recovery" from addictions of their own in turn become addiction clinicians, and may bring their own experiences and empathy into play in a way that helps them make a connection with teenagers. However, only the proper education and training qualifies a clinician to identify your teenager's immediate needs and know what treatment will meet those needs.

Psychiatrists don't all undergo specialized addiction training, and their general psychiatric schooling doesn't make them addiction experts. Some social workers, psychologists, and psychiatrists are superior addiction clinicians because of their training and experience, while others have no experience or interest in working with addiction. Child psychiatrists and child psychologists, for instance, don't necessarily have the requisite preparation. No matter what his or her other qualifications, however, your teenager's addiction counselor must have formal addiction training and treatment experience to be truly effective.

FINDING HELP

Personal recommendations are a great way to locate a therapist who can evaluate your substance-using teen, provide care, and find treatment centers. A good place to start is with your pediatrician or family doctor, in the same way you might ask her for the name of a good dermatologist or physical therapy facility. Your doctor can access professional resources for finding addiction clinicians and programs by exploring these resources for you. You may be reluctant to reveal addiction concerns to your doctor, but don't let this stand in the way of tapping one of your best sources of information. Most pediatricians have seen drug-involved teenagers so often that they're decent clinicians themselves. Doctors should view the problem as just another medical issue, as opposed to something shameful. Some pediatricians even specialize in treating substance-using teenagers.

Also ask every trusted friend and family member where to find a good addiction clinician or treatment program for your teenager. It probably won't be difficult, once you start asking around, to discover someone you know who has overcome an addiction problem. Without going into details, ask her some questions: Where did you go for help? Whom would you recommend to evaluate my teenager? Do you know where there's a good AA group for teenagers? An Al-Anon group for me?

School counselors can also lend a hand in finding addiction clinicians, programs, and general guidance for your teenager. Even if your teenager isn't yet having problems with schoolwork, you can contact his school counselor—anonymously if you wish—to find help. Be advised, though, that counselors may be required to report students who have, or may have, a drug problem, but I have yet to hear of a school counselor who won't immediately provide all of her contacts to any parent or student who asks, even anonymously.

You can even find a good clinician or program through your health insurance company. This is an especially good approach if you want a therapist or facility that accepts your health insurance. Start by calling your insurer's toll-free number or browsing its website to generate a list of addiction treatment professionals. Take your list to your doctor, relatives, friends, or school counselor and ask whom they've heard good things about and whom they would recommend.

You can also check out the therapists you hear about from any source by Googling them, but take information that you find online with a grain of salt. The Internet can provide a wealth of addiction facts and treatment contacts, but it is also rife with use-less—and even some very bad—information. You'll need to inter-pret your findings yourself. Remember that some websites are just advertisements for treatment facilities: Addiction professionals call them "cowboy websites" because they're designed to "round 'em up" into a particular program. Beware of websites that suggest only one facility or only one method of treatment. Choose a treatment center with care and with the assistance of a qualified clinician who knows your child. Check the Reader's Resources list at the back of this book for some excellent websites.

INPATIENT VS. OUTPATIENT PROGRAMS FOR YOUR TEENAGER

Parents often ask me whether their substance-using teenager should enter an inpatient or outpatient treatment program in addition to or instead of getting individual therapy. Depending on your teenager's needs, either type of program can be enormously beneficial. The key to deciding what treatment your teenager needs is to maintain a measured response to her problems. In this often-baffling scenario, it's up to you to determine which type of treatment might have the best chances of success. In order to make the decision about which treatment—if any—your teenager needs, get professional advice from a knowledgeable clinician who understands the full gamut of addiction treatment options available.

I've served as director of inpatient facilities and occasionally refer my patients to them, but I strongly believe that inpatient treat-ment should be used only when absolutely necessary. If she's bing-ing on cocaine and cannot seem to stop, an inpatient program is probably the best treatment option, but if she's smoking marijuana occasionally, inpatient treatment would be worse-than-useless over-kill. Inpatient programs carry their own set of potential risks, such as the fact that your teenager's training in coping skills can be weak because it takes place in an unrealistic, protected environment that doesn't reflect the challenges of the "real world." Of course, some-times inpatient treatment is absolutely necessary to keep your teen-ager safe, or if outpatient treatment has failed.

Be aware, also, that both inpatient and outpatient treatment (and even Alcoholics Anonymous) can have an unintended consequence: it will expose your teenager to "expert" information about drugs and alcohol delivered by others with a lot more experience. Still, for certain teenagers, the upsides of treatment programs far outweigh this potential downside. Frankly, your teenager can find drugs or using-buddies anywhere, and the vast majority of those who attend a treatment program or an AA meeting are doing their best to stay sober.

Generally speaking, treatment facilities should be absolutely forthright about their usual treatment methods, their experience with the specific sorts of problems your teenager is facing, and the coverage (or lack thereof) offered by your particular insurance plan. You may not be an expert in addiction treatment, but you can and should expect to have your questions answered in a way that you can understand. Now that you know what to look for, how do you go about finding the right clinician to evaluate and treat your substance-using teenager, and how do you research treatment programs?

WHAT ABOUT ALCOHOLICS ANONYMOUS?

Your substance-using teenager should *definitely* check out AA or another peer-led support group, such as NA (Narcotics Anonymous), MA (Marijuana Anonymous), or PA (Pills Anonymous). I recommend that she give one or more of these groups a test drive by attending several different meetings geared toward young people. There, she'll meet other teenagers who face similar challenges and see how the program can work for her. In the best of circumstances, your teenager will hear the stories of others who are successfully confronting their addiction, and learn how they avoid the particular pitfalls of teenage peer pressure to use drugs and alcohol. I've found that many teenagers who at first say they wouldn't be caught dead at an AA or other peer-led meeting ultimately decide that the group has a lot to offer, and they end up going to meetings on a regular basis.

I don't believe that peer-led support groups are the only answer to addiction, or that they can replace professional treatment (and they don't claim to). Plus, they aren't the right way to go for every teenager in every situation. Attending meetings can be problematic if your teenager's therapist disagrees with the philosophy of a given peer-led group. (If that happens, try to understand exactly what the concern is, and try to find a group that is consistent with your teenager's professional treatment.) Nonetheless, I've found that AA and similar peer-led support groups can be enormously beneficial in most cases. Likewise, many outpatient and inpatient treatment centers recognize the value of peer-led support groups and require that their clients attend AA or similar meetings—for good reason.

Peer-led support groups help teenagers acknowledge the tremendous power of addictive substances and show them how to rely on certain time-tested strategies for resisting that power. Many members have life-changing revelations about what really matters. Perhaps even more importantly, peer-led support groups provide a highly supportive environment for teenagers who are trying to attain or maintain sobriety. At meetings, your teenager can start building the positive friendships and substance-free relationships that can smooth her road to recovery. If she attends meetings regularly and participates in the "fellowship" sessions afterward, your teenager will gain a social network of highly empathetic friends—and a 24/7 crisis-support system. These can become permanent resources for the rest of your teenager's life, in a way that an individual therapist or treatment center cannot.

You might worry that peer support meetings will introduce your teenager to other addicted teens with whom she'll use or buy illicit substances. Truth is, she can find those kids anywhere. As a rule, though, recovery meetings are filled with people who are maintaining sobriety or working hard to get there. It's possible that your teenager might come across drugs or booze or active users at a meeting, but even so, the prevailing ethos is one of sobriety and support for living a productive, engaged life. I've seen peer-led support groups help teenagers in ways that no therapist or nonaddict ever could.

"I WON'T GO!"

Substance-using teenagers often argue that they don't need to quit alcohol or drugs or to get treatment, because they're only drinking or drugging in rebellion against their parents or other authority figures. This extremely common attitude, that self-destructive substance abuse is a way to reject society's norms or "fight the power," is transparent nonsense. You are the judge of whether and when your teenager needs treatment. How should you react if your teenager refuses to go into treatment? I recommend four strategies.

WHEN YOUR TEENAGER REFUSES TREATMENT

- Be ready to call 911.
- Get help for yourself.
- Set up logical consequences.
- Stay in the game!

First, if your teenager shows any of the potentially catastrophic signs of a substance use problem, such as suicidal thoughts, ongoing cocaine or heroin use or injecting drugs, you must take action immediately! Regardless of what your teenager believes or insists, you might need to send him to involuntary treatment by calling 911 (responders will take him to the hospital) or by getting him ordered to an inpatient program by a judge. If your teenager is highly resistant, these might be your only options for getting your child into treatment.

More likely, your situation won't be so dire, and you can move directly to the second strategy: get help for yourself. You're so emotionally close to your substance-using teenager that your judgment is off. Are you overreacting? Underreacting? Your emotional state can make it hard for you to tell how much danger your teenager's in, what kind of help he needs and how quickly he needs it. An addiction clinician's objective, experienced outlook is invaluable in helping you formulate the best possible response to your defiant teenager. In my practice, I spend a lot of time rehearsing parents on exactly what to say in this situation.

Tough Talk Dialog: "I Just Don't Want to Leave My Friends."

Anna: Sam, Dad and I talked with your therapist and she really thinks you should go to the outpatient program we heard about.

Sam: No way. That place is a joke. I'll talk to Dr. Collins, but there's no way I'm going to waste my time in some stupid program.

Dad: Well, you've continued drinking when we all agreed it was dangerous and you needed to stop, and it really does seem like you need extra help. What don't you like about the program?

Sam: I just don't want to leave my friends. Going after school three times a week? Are you kidding me? That's our hangout time.

Anna: We understand that, but this is really important and, actually, it's a step down from what Dr. Collins said about maybe needing to go to an inpatient program—that would really be leaving your friends!

Sam: Whoa! Are you threatening me that you're going to send me away?

Dad: No, it's not a threat. The reality is that if you aren't safe, the next step would be an inpatient place, but more important than that is what could happen if you keep drinking—if you maim or kill yourself, you'll leave your friends permanently!

Sam: Please, Dad. You're being so dramatic.

Dad: Maybe I am, but we can't ignore the reality that you've put yourself in some real danger by getting alcohol poisoning last week and being in the car when James was driving drunk and all that.

Sam: You'd really send me away?

Anna: To help you, yes. All we're asking for now is that you go to the outpatient program for six weeks. It makes a lot of sense.

Sam: Not to me.

Dad: You really don't have a choice on this one, son.

Anna and Roger have learned how to take the right approach to Sam's unwillingness to get more treatment for his alcohol problem. They stay on-message, avoid being drawn into unnecessary conflict, and agree to disagree about the outpatient program—but insist on it nonetheless.

Peer-led support groups like Al-Anon (for adults who love an addicted person) and Alateen (for teenagers who love an addicted person) can also help you manage a teenager who's refusing treatment. They can provide a wealth of information about strategies for getting stubborn teenagers the help they need. At meetings, you'll hear stories of families similar to your own and how they deal with their problems. You'll probably also learn about the importance of setting reasonable boundaries and limits for your teenager.

This is the third strategy: setting up "logical consequences." Addiction counselor Dick Schaefer explains this strategy in his book, *Choices & Consequences: What to Do When a Teenager Uses Alcohol/Drugs: A Step-by-Step System That Really Works.* Without your intervention, your teenager's substance-using behavior results in "natural consequences," such as hangovers and drunk-driving arrests. You can add even more downsides to his behavior by imposing your own negative logical consequences in response to his actions.

It's extremely important that the logical consequences you establish for your teenager are: (1) proportionate to the behavior that brings them about; (2) set up in advance; and (3) enforceable. If the consequences don't meet all three of those criteria, there's little chance that they'll work. For instance, you can enforce the preset consequence of taking away the car keys if you smell marijuana on your teenager. Or you might tell him that he'll have to have an appointment with an addiction counselor if he gets drunk again—and then make sure he goes.

I've worked with many families whose teenagers absolutely refused to undergo treatment until the parents, with my guidance and support, started withdrawing privileges and enforcing logical consequences for that refusal. For example, a high school senior named Eli refused to go to school, smoked an enormous amount of marijuana, and refused to get treatment. He ignored the pleas of his parents, teachers—and even a few friends—to put down the marijuana and go back to school. Eli really didn't do much of anything, even come down to dinner with his family, but he did enjoy a few things, such as playing Xbox® 360 and watching pro football games. When his parents threatened to take away his video games and television if he didn't at least try outpatient treatment, Eli paid no attention. When his father actually confiscated his Xbox®, Eli was enraged and threatened to leave the house. Together, his parents calmly told him that, while they didn't want him to leave, they insisted that he go to outpatient treatment or else they would send him to inpatient treatment. After a standoff of several days, Eli finally consented to come see me.

At first, he did little but complain about his parents' unreasonable demands and repeat his refusal to do anything about his marijuana use. Eventually, though, after another week and a half of testing his parents' resolve, Eli agreed to enter an inpatient treatment facility. After a difficult first week there, he was surprised to find himself on the road to sobriety. Though Eli felt that he was forced into treatment, he was actually glad of it!

Although it's far from certain, logical consequences such as these give you the best odds of getting your teenager to accept treatment. The relentless logic of your position may break through to him, but perhaps more importantly, the reasonableness of what you're doing will allow you to continue doing it much longer than you would be able to follow through on exaggerated or catastrophic consequences.

You're probably realizing by now that you're in for a very long haul. This is where the fourth strategy comes into play: Stay in the game! Backing off from your teenager's substance problem—because you're exhausted, or you don't think things will ever change, or for whatever reason—is tantamount to abandoning him to his addiction. You might not mean to ignore his needs, but that's what will happen if you don't stay in the game. Don't avoid the issue by closing your eyes to ongoing damage or by shipping your kid off to rehab for a minor problem. Both of these are disproportionate moves that have more to do with minimizing your anxieties than with helping your teenager. Taking yourself out of the game this way leaves your teenager to his own devices—and his own mess.

POINTS TO REMEMBER

- An addiction clinician can help you determine the best approach to your teenager's treatment.
- Carefully research the qualifications and experience of your teenager's addiction clinician.
- Make sure your teenager's treatment is proportionate to his problem.
- Use my four recommended strategies if your teenager refuses treatment.
- Act immediately in "911" situations.

Chapter 11

OUTPATIENT TREATMENT FOR YOUR SUBSTANCE-USING TEENAGER

The great thing in this world is not so much where you stand, as in what direction you're moving.

—Oliver Wendell Holmes

f it is warranted, good outpatient treatment will provide drug- or alcohol-using teenagers with a set of adaptive skills that she can use to defend herself against substance use, drug, and alcohol cravings, as well as life's difficulties. It will teach her how to handle her cravings with confidence, forcefulness, and ease. Equipped with these skills, your teenager will be a lot like Bruce Lee in one of his martial arts movies: when the bad guys attack in seemingly endless ways, he defends himself with a grace and certainty that leaves them unconscious or dead, and slips away quietly.

Representing a middle ground between weekly therapist visits and full-time treatment in inpatient facilities, outpatient treatment is the best option for most substance-using teenagers who need more help than an individual therapist can provide. I recommend it for the majority of my patients who need further assistance.

WHAT TO EXPECT FROM OUTPATIENT TREATMENT

By treating your substance-using teenager on a daily basis, an outpatient treatment center can teach her how to face ordinary life stressors. It will take day after day of practice for her to learn how to respond to everyday challenges such as peer pressure, school troubles, and conflicts at home. Outpatient treatment centers support sobriety by providing your teenager with daily support while she remains immersed in the inevitable pressures of her life.

High-quality outpatient programs offer teenagers a comprehensive package of services designed to pull them away from drugs and alcohol and push them back into a gratifying, engaged life. When enrolled in an outpatient treatment center, your teenager will attend group therapy, get drug tested, and start getting involved with peer support groups like AA. Optimally, the treatment package will also include individual therapy, family meetings, and extended psychological assessment, if necessary.

While your teenager is going through an outpatient treatment program, he will probably meet with an in-house clinician of some sort every week. This clinician can coordinate all the moving parts of the comprehensive treatment plan designed by your teenager's team. In the best of circumstances, your teenager's program clinician will become a trusted advisor who can remain on the scene after the more intensive aspects of treatment have concluded.

An outpatient facility might call itself an "intensive outpatient program" (IOP), to underscore that its concentrated services are just one step less rigorous than inpatient treatment. This sort of program delivers several hours per day of treatment services and access to specialists such as licensed drug counselors, social workers, and nurses. A good outpatient facility should have a strong affiliation with an inpatient treatment program, so that patients can be transferred there quickly if necessary. For the patient who exhibits psychiatric symptoms like suicidal thinking, or who is dangerously intoxicated, or withdrawing from alcohol, rapid inpatient admission can get her back on her feet quickly.

Outpatient programs are indispensable for teenagers who are readjusting to the real world after being discharged from an inpatient program. In the outside world, drugs and alcohol are just as available as they were before their inpatient treatment, and an IOP can make the transition easier and more successful.

HOW TO CHOOSE AN OUTPATIENT TREATMENT PROGRAM

Selecting an outpatient program is much easier if you ask the advice of an addiction clinician who knows your teenager, preferably the therapist he's already seeing. An informed professional can lend a hand in determining which services to seek, and will know the reputations of nearby treatment centers. With any luck, your teenager's clinician will have relationships with some of them. Another good place to start is with your health insurance provider, which should have a list of facilities in your area that are both state certified and covered by your policy.

Outpatient treatment programs vary considerably. Research the specific services offered at the facilities you're considering and make sure those services match your teenager's needs. Different teenagers have different needs: Yours may require an on-site psychiatrist to manage medications, while others may need only a built-in peer group of sober teenagers. Still, other kids may require daily drug testing or an on-site nurse to manage a separate medical problem. There's no one-size-fits-all program, so have a clear picture of what your substance-using teenager needs when you look into outpatient programs. Seek out programs that offer a comprehensive program overseen by a trained and licensed professional.

FINDING THE RIGHT OUTPATIENT PROGRAM: QUESTIONS TO ASK

- How many hours per day do clients spend at the center?
- Do the group sessions focus on education? Confrontation? Support?
- Does the center provide individual therapy?
- Does the center provide drug and alcohol testing?

- Can my teenager's outpatient therapist continue treating him while he's enrolled?
- What's the policy regarding clients who slip and use drugs or alcohol?

There's no single right answer to any of these questions, but asking them can enlighten you about a treatment center's philosophy and approach, and can help you judge whether or not it's a good fit with your child's needs. For instance, the protocols for dealing with a teenager who slips back to drug or alcohol use vary from center to center. Some programs are relatively lenient and regard slips as part of recovery; their strategy is to try to identify the triggers that provoked the slip and to prevent further relapse. Other facilities take a hard line, with a "one-strike" policy that dictates discharge of any teenager who slips, and recommends that he enter, or go back into, inpatient treatment. There are also facilities that lie somewhere in the middle. No approach is perfect, and you should pick a facility based on your teenager's specific needs. A clinician who knows your teenager well should help with your selection of a facility.

IF YOUR TEENAGER SAYS "NO" TO OUTPATIENT TREATMENT

Of course, your teenager may not want to go into—or stay in—an outpatient treatment program. If that's the case, hear him out and learn what the problem is.

Tough Talk Dialog: "Outpatient Makes Me Want to Use—It's Stupid!"

Billy: OK Mom, I went to Fresh Start all week and I want to talk to you about it like we said.

Roseanne: Sure. What did you think of it?

Billy: Not much. I don't think it does any good. It's the same thing all day, blah, blah, blah.

Roseanne: Well, all your drug screens have been negative. That's got to be a good sign!

Billy:	*Yeah, but that's not because of Fresh Start. I don't want to use—I told you.*
Roseanne:	*Well, it's really great you haven't used. Doesn't Fresh Start help you with that?*
Billy:	*Nope. I go there and I want to use. The kids there always talk about drugs and I get cravings. Plus some of them have relapsed. I could even use drugs with them!*
Roseanne:	*Well, that's a first! You felt like using drugs and you didn't—that's not easy. Did the staff support you in that?*
Billy:	*No! We just sit around in the idiotic meetings, and when I say I want to use, it's the other kids who tell me to hang in there and wait for the craving to stop. That's all they say.*
Roseanne:	*So the other kids support you?*
Billy:	*Yeah… the ones who aren't using! Outpatient makes me want to use. It's stupid! We just sit there like morons for sixty minutes, and by the time the meeting is over I'm too bored to use.*
Roseanne:	*Well, something is going right. You have a craving and it passes.*
Billy:	*Do I still have to go there?*
Roseanne:	*Yes. It seems to me like you're hanging out with the right kids there—the ones who aren't using. I know it's painful and boring, but you're definitely doing the right thing.*

Roseanne lets Billy say his piece and doesn't disagree that outpatient treatment can be boring, but she points out the positives and insists that he keep going.

SHOULD MY TEENAGER'S THERAPIST BE INVOLVED?
This is a tricky question, which you should consider even before your substance-using teenager enters an outpatient program. The

bottom line is that both your teenager's outpatient program and her therapist must focus on the best ways to help her stop using alcohol and addictive drugs, and to get her life back on track.

Some outpatient facilities allow teenagers to continue seeing their outside therapist while attending the program. They work quite well with these therapists, maintaining a good flow of information in both directions and gladly discharge teenagers back into the care of their therapist when they complete the program. Other outpatient programs take the stance, not unreasonably, that their clients' interests are best served by a treatment plan that's developed and followed by clinicians working under one roof. If a client keeps appointments with her outside therapist while enrolled in the outpatient program, the thinking goes, discrepancies between her providers' perspectives will inevitably arise and create counterproductive chaos.

The right approach depends mostly on your teenager's outside therapist. A competent addiction therapist will understand the value of maintaining harmony with your teenager's structured, time-intensive outpatient program, even if the program's point of view isn't entirely shared. However, to the outside therapist who's not experienced in addiction, some of the program's recommendations and policies might seem a bit odd. If, for instance, his therapeutic focus is on helping your teenager to develop insight into her problems, an outpatient program's focus on behavior over root causes might be off-putting. If her outside therapist has little experience or training in addiction, you should be looking for another therapist anyway!

As parents, step back and make sure that your teenager's individual therapist and her outpatient program stay focused—and in agreement—on the long-term well-being of your teenager. If her outside therapist won't work with the outpatient program you have selected, then your teenager may need to take a break from psychotherapy while she's in the program. If an outpatient program insists that only its personnel will be permitted to provide her therapy, explore the implications for her treatment: Would she continue working with the program's therapist after she finishes the outpatient program? Would her outside therapist pick up where the program leaves off?

POINTS TO REMEMBER

- Outpatient treatment is preferable to inpatient treatment unless inpatient is absolutely necessary.
- Make sure your teenager's outpatient program has the right mix of services.
- The outpatient program and your teenager's outside clinician must communicate.
- Outpatient programs should have easy access to inpatient treatment facilities.

Chapter 12

INPATIENT TREATMENT FOR YOUR SUBSTANCE-USING TEENAGER

In the middle of difficulty lies opportunity.

—Albert Einstein

Having worked in and supervised several inpatient addiction-treatment facilities, I know that inpatient rehabilitation can be very productive for some substance-using teenagers. I also know that you absolutely should not send your teenager to an inpatient facility unless she meets specific criteria as determined by a knowledgeable addiction clinician. Sometimes the sheltered environment offered by an inpatient facility is advantageous, though you should question any knee-jerk advice to have your teenager admitted to one.

Inpatient treatment, while necessary in certain circumstances, is counterproductive overkill when an outpatient program will suffice. The environment within the safe, supportive confines of an inpatient facility is unlike anything your teenager encounters out in the "real world," so she learns her drug-refusal strategies in the total absence of any actual cues to use. She has to figure out how to build on those strategies and develop ways to deal with challenges after she's discharged. Her tricky reentry into everyday life can put her sobriety in jeopardy.

WHEN TO CHOOSE INPATIENT TREATMENT

Your teenager needs inpatient addiction treatment only under severe, unambiguous conditions: First, it's only necessary if he also has a serious psychiatric condition or is thinking about suicide. Second, take him to an inpatient facility only if he's using substances in a potentially lethal or medically dangerous manner (for instance, if he uses cocaine, experiences alcohol poisoning, or is at risk of overdosing on opioids). Third, he requires inpatient care if his attempts at outpatient treatment haven't worked.

When inpatient rehabilitation is required, it doesn't represent a failure on your teenager's, or anyone's, part. Like psychotherapy and outpatient treatment, it's simply another option—albeit a time-consuming and usually expensive option—to help your teenager. Look at inpatient addiction treatment in the same way that you look at hospitalization for any other medical condition. Your doctor might recommend hospitalization, for instance, to provide more intensive therapy for an infection that doesn't clear up with home treatment. Similarly, being admitted for inpatient addiction care for a second, third, or fourth time, isn't a disaster, but an acknowledgement that other treatment isn't succeeding and more intensive care is needed. Admission or readmission to inpatient care can be the turning point for your teenager to begin rebuilding his life.

WHAT TO EXPECT FROM DETOX AND REHAB

Detox and rehab are two separate components of inpatient care. A doctor should assess your teenager medically at the start of her inpatient treatment to determine if she should first undergo detoxification, or detox. As the term implies, detox allows her to withdraw safely from the substance(s) she's been using, Teenagers are much less likely to require detox than are adults, who often have been addicted for many years.

The detox process is usually supported by medications, because withdrawing from alcohol can be fatal, while withdrawing from opioids such as heroin is often painful, but not dangerous. Medication can make withdrawal less dangerous and prevent the physical agony that can cause your teenager to go back to her substance of choice. Detox itself isn't addiction treatment, but a precursor to treatment; ideally, your teenager's detox facility will refer her to rehab treatment immediately after her withdrawal.

Your teenager's inpatient treatment usually begins in rehabilitation, or rehab. Although the programs offered by inpatient rehabilitation centers vary, all share a few common traits. Many follow a twenty-eight-day plan created in the 1960s by Minnesota-based Hazelden (www.hazelden.org), one of the world's largest and most respected addiction treatment centers. Known as the "Minnesota Model" or "28-Day Model," the structured rehab program is designed to take addicts through a clearly defined course of group and individual treatment and bring them into the early stages of sobriety. As in AA's 12-step paradigm, Minnesota Model programs have traditionally viewed psychiatric medication skeptically, but they have recently become much more inclusive. The model has become the standard for inpatient facilities, although these sorts of facilities now face increasing pressure to demonstrate their program's effectiveness and the necessity for the relatively long stay it requires.

Inpatient facilities offer the sort of intensive, nearly around-the-clock treatment that even the most intensive outpatient programs can't match. Your teenager may very well need such concentrated treatment in order to get started on the road to recovery. At all rehab centers, your teenager stays in the facility night and day as long as she's under treatment. This approach eliminates easily obtainable drugs or alcohol from the picture, a factor that's absolutely necessary for some addicted teenagers. (At most rehabilitation facilities, doors to the outside world remain unlocked, but some centers also have provisions for holding teenagers against their will when necessary.) In addition to a substance-free environment, inpatient programs also have a requirement that your teenager do almost everything with her fellow patients, such as attend group therapy, eat meals, and spend her free time. This collective living experience is designed to foster group cohesion and mutual support, as teenagers help one another through the harrowing experience of stopping drug and alcohol use.

NEGOTIATING FOR HEALTH INSURANCE COVERAGE

The twenty-eight-day inpatient treatment blueprint has come into such widespread use that many health insurance companies now expect to cover no more than twenty-eight days of inpatient therapy for substance abuse. Some have taken this policy one step further, arguing that there's no magic in twenty-eight days, and while some addicts need that much treatment, others need far less. As a result, the length of your teenager's inpatient stay will most likely be tied to her specific needs, rather than to a preset number of days.

Make sure your teenager gets as many days of treatment as she needs. This is usually negotiated between her treatment facility, her outside clinician, and your health insurance company. Many addiction treatment centers know how to make a strong case with insurers, and can back up their treatment philosophy with published literature and established criteria. When it's your turn to negotiate with your insurer, don't hesitate to argue forcefully for what you believe your teenager needs; you'll probably have to pull out the big guns in order to collect the benefits you've paid for. I have seen some parents enlist an attorney, or appeal to their state's insurance commissioner if they feel their insurance company is not treating them fairly.

WILDERNESS EXPERIENCES

A relatively new industry of inpatient programs provides addiction treatment to teenagers in wilderness settings. These wilderness experiences are for the most part designed to assist teenagers who are involved with drugs and alcohol, and sometimes those with dual diagnoses of addiction plus eating disorders or other psychiatric problems. The idea behind them is to take your teenager out of his comfort zone and combine varying degrees of treatment with an intense nature experience to bring about lasting change. This unique experience can be described as a "rite of passage," a transformational process that is difficult to find in our fast-paced, modern society." The website is now http://aspeneducation.crchealth.com/outdoor-edu

Only loosely regulated by federal, state, and local governments, wilderness programs vary widely in the quality of the treatment they provide, the credentials of their employees, their licensing status, and their ability to respond quickly to addiction or psychiatric emergencies. Exercise caution in reviewing the services offered by wilderness programs, and make sure that any program you're considering has the resources available to handle your child's problems.

If wilderness programs in the United States are inadequately regulated, those in foreign countries are even less well regulated: The US Department of State has weighed in with concerns about them. In 2008, it issued an explicit statement that it has no control over such programs and can inspect them only on an informal basis. The most worrisome part of the statement noted the following:

> The facilities can be located in relatively remote areas, restrict the minor child's contact with the outside world, and employ a system of graduated levels of earned privileges and punishments. The Department of State has, at various times, received complaints about nutrition, housing, education, health issues, and methods of punishment used at some facilities.

Use extra caution when considering a wilderness experience-type inpatient program for your teenager!

PERSUADING YOUR TEENAGER TO GO TO INPATIENT TREATMENT

A frequent argument against inpatient treatment—and one that you might hear from your substance-using teenager—is that it removes the addict from the realities he's trying to master. Inpatient facilities are free of drugs and alcohol, provide emotional support, and shield patients from the real-life cues that trigger drug use. How can your teenager learn to handle the challenges of everyday living when he's being treated in a bubble? In some ways this criticism is valid, but it ignores the many benefits of inpatient programs. Maintaining sobriety out in the world is, of course, the goal for your teenager, but if he can't seem to reach that goal he might need a jump start from intensive inpatient care.

Tough Talk Dialog: "It Isn't Real Life!"

Alex: *Are you kidding me, Dad? I'm not going to inpatient. That's crazy!*

Dad: *Well, it can't be any crazier than what's going on in your life now—you've been drunk every night this week, and missed most of your classes!*

Alex: *All the guys are doing it.*

Dad: *Oh, please, son. You don't even believe that yourself. "The guys," as you say, are all worried sick about you. Bobby called me last week to say you're out of control. He's really scared for you.*

Alex: *Yeah, I know, but inpatient is ridiculous. It isn't real life. My life is here. Nothing is going to change if I go there—it will all be the same when I get home.*

Dad: *Yes, it will, but the intake counselor from the inpatient place told me that you would at least get a break from the constant pressure you're under, and that you could learn some strategies for saying "no" to the booze. It just looks like you're not managing on your own here and when we went to outpatient you never went back.*

Alex: *I gotta do something, but I just don't think checking in to rehab is it. That would be like giving up.*

Dad: *I don't think it's giving up or anything like that. I think it's taking the bull by the horns. What you're doing now—nothing—isn't working, so you have to try some other strategy.*

Alex: *What do you mean it's not working? I'm getting along! You don't want me to miss any more class, do you?*

Dad: *Of course I don't, but you miss most of your classes now, and you'll miss more than a few classes if you don't get some help now. I'm worried about you losing your future!*

Alex: *Dramatic much, Dad? It's only alcohol. It's not like I'm using drugs or something, so I don't need rehab.*

Dad: *It is only alcohol, but the alcohol can destroy your life in the same way that drugs can. It doesn't really matter what you're using, only that you're harming yourself!*

Alex: *Well... it almost makes sense when you say it that way.*

Roger agrees with Alex where he can, but also makes a case for inpatient treatment. He prepped for this conversation with an intake counselor, so he's not dissuaded by Alex's arguments: the unreality of the inpatient setting, the prospect of missing classes(!) and the "it's just alcohol" argument. Alex needs inpatient care!

CAN WE FORCE OUR TEENAGER TO GO TO INPATIENT TREATMENT?

Short answer: not very easily. No parent relishes the idea of forcing his child into inpatient treatment, but your family's situation might reach the point where you have no other choice. Your teenager might not have "hit bottom" yet, but you don't have to wait until she does. Her bottom might be far lower than you think it is. Just be sure to try everything short of brute force before you play the coercion card. There's a lot of ground between allowing your teenager to suffer and hustling her into a car with a couple of beefy "assistants."

The middle ground includes setting logical consequences (see chapter 10) and consistently putting pressure on your teenager to accept treatment. Although I don't recommend that every conversation be about accepting treatment, this pressure should include frequent conversations about getting help, as well as calls to other family members and close friends. You don't have to stage a formal intervention to reach out to grandparents, uncles, and cousins for support. Similarly, school counselors, clergy, and coaches are often willing to help and are experienced in dealing with troubled young people. Whatever you do, don't keep the situation a secret—any feelings of embarrassment or shame that stop you from talking about your teenager's substance use will simply allow the problem to fester.

Only if, despite everything you've done, your teenager just won't give up drugs or alcohol, or if she obstinately refuses to participate in treatment, should you to consider forcing the issue. Physically compelling your teenager into an inpatient facility is a last resort, but in some cases it's a necessity and, indeed, your obligation.

At the most extreme end of the coercion spectrum, when your teenager has managed to defeat all of your efforts, you might be able to bring in a third party who has the power to take even stronger measures. Only a police officer or a judge can deprive a person of her liberty; the police can do so only briefly, while the courts can order longer-term detention. Going to the authorities is a terribly difficult step to take, and a categorical last resort, but unfortunately, in a tiny minority of cases it's the only way to get your teenager into treatment.

When I'm counseling parents who have no choice but to consider this radical tactic, I support them in finding programs for legally mandated teenagers—programs that are accredited, experienced, and stay well within the parameters of the law. I'm also committed to helping families retain the services of an attorney who specializes in mental health issues. Ideally, with the assistance of your teenager's clinician, hire a qualified attorney before you contact those who will physically take your teenager to treatment. Do the same sort of thorough research into programs that accept legally mandated teenagers.

Legitimate treatment programs are very careful to adhere to the applicable laws, and they scrupulously inform parents about what inpatient facilities can and cannot do when teenagers are legally ordered to undergo treatment.

Take some comfort in the fact that abundant research shows that addicts who are coerced into treatment do as well as those who choose it of their own accord. Almost everyone who enters inpatient addiction treatment voluntarily has had her arm twisted in some way, whether by a parent, work supervisor, or therapist. As an addiction therapist, I have witnessed countless instances in which a teenager has been forced—physically or otherwise—into treatment, and the end result has been excellent. Sometimes teenagers actually thank their parents for making them enter a program, but even if they don't, you can assure yourself that you've done absolutely everything to protect your teenager.

A TALE OF CARING CONCERN

One teenager with whom I worked, had serious problems that required her parents to take extreme measures. Although Barbara had never had even a sip of alcohol until she was fourteen, by the time I met her two years later she was a hard-partying, rebellious teenager who spent most of her weekend evenings drunk, high on cocaine, or both. When Barbara started snorting cocaine the summer before her junior year of high school, her parents were frightened out of their wits. She had lost weight, seemed sexually promiscuous, and had snuck off to New York City on several occasions, for reasons her parents never found out.

The one time I met Barbara, I was immediately convinced that her life was in danger. I put together a plan to get her into inpatient treatment right away, but needless to say, she refused any help I offered and vociferously rejected the same sort of help from her parents. She even said that she would run away if her parents tried to make her go to treatment, which was, of course, exactly what they planned to do.

After securing a bed in a treatment center several hours away, Barbara's parents bundled her into the car on a Saturday morning with the pretext of taking her to her friend Ilana's house. Ilana agreed that Barbara was in desperate need of treatment and had agreed to phone her during the trip to provide some comfort and support. After driving her across town, Barbara's parents kept going, all the way to the treatment facility's front gate. The trip to the facility was enormously painful for her parents, who had to listen to her angry denial, threats to jump out of the car, and eventual weeping. Yet they knew that misleading Barbara, enduring a horrible episode, and even risking that their daughter might try to run away were worth it, because their actions probably saved her life.

POINTS TO REMEMBER

- Do not send your teenager to an inpatient treatment facility except under specific, severe circumstances.
- Be very cautious about wilderness programs.
- Your teenager might need to be persuaded to enter an inpatient program.
- Coerce your teenager into inpatient treatment only after you've tried every possible way to persuade him.
- Exhaust every other possible means of coercion before turning to the legal system.

Chapter 13

AFTERCARE: THE NEXT STEP AFTER INTENSIVE TREATMENT

Maybe I'm not an alcoholic anymore.

—Anonymous

Aftercare is what happens after your teenager's drug or alcohol crisis has passed and he graduates from his intensive outpatient program or comes home from inpatient treatment. When the initial panic fades and he completes the first phase of his rehabilitation, he'll definitely need this follow-up treatment. Your teenager will be ready to integrate back into real life, but the transition will be perilous. Unfortunately, in the first few days to weeks after full-on treatment ends teenagers often get lost, let down their guard, and relapse. The goal of aftercare is to prevent slips or relapses, and to promote your teenager's ongoing learning, growth, and recovery.

Aftercare is best conceived of as a permanent need. The recovering addict will need to keep his eye on the ball *forever*. This isn't depressing news—it's a very positive thing! I know plenty of recovering addicts who have moved on to very rich lives, with gratifying jobs, loving families, and exciting new experiences. It takes continuous vigilance to achieve this success and to keep the addiction locked in its box.

AFTERCARE IN ACTION

Addiction is a chronic condition, one that your teenager will need to deal with for the rest of her life. In this respect, addiction is like any other chronic disease. Ongoing treatment of a person who has diabetes or high blood pressure aims to make her life as normal and free of medical hassles as possible, and so it is for addiction. Aftercare will help your teenager move to a stage of recovery in which she can balance the need for treatment with the need to get back to school, relationships, and regular day-to-day living.

Your teenager will be returning to her old life in some respects, but she'll also be redefining it. As an AA aphorism puts it, she'll be working to change the people, places, and things that shaped her lifestyle as a substance user. This process is hard enough for adults, and nearly impossible for most teenagers, but your teenager's aftercare plan can address the most difficult parts of making those changes.

The first goal of aftercare—preventing slips or relapses—is best achieved when there's a direct connection between intensive treatment and the return to normal life. Before your teenager leaves her inpatient or outpatient program, her addiction clinician should design and put in place an aftercare plan. Insist that the plan be individualized based on your teenager's drug of choice, social skills, living environment, and understanding of addiction and recovery. The plan can and should be modified over time, depending on your teenager's progress, slips, and increasing maturity. The plan should set a specific date for her first therapy appointment and schedule her first peer-led support group meeting. I always ask that a teenager who's being discharged from an inpatient or outpatient program meet with me the day she's sent home: I want to get her reengaged with the sober world while the engaging is good.

Aftercare should include psychotherapy with a clinician who's knowledgeable about and experienced in addiction treatment. Your teenager will benefit greatly from this partnership as she learns to function without the tremendous emotional support she received in intensive treatment. Learning how to deal with frustration, anger, and even joy alongside the usual give-and-take of everyday life, all without drugs or alcohol, is difficult to say the least. During this process, therapy can be a great resource and emotional backup. In addition, a therapist can coordinate the many elements of the care that your teenager is receiving, and can conduct urine drug screens to make sure the aftercare treatment is working.

Peer-led support groups such as Alcoholics Anonymous are another essential part of aftercare. By attending meetings geared toward young people, your teenager can start building the social relationships and learning the habits she needs to live a sober life. The social networking that takes place at most AA-style meetings is one of the most powerful tools that your teenager can use in her recovery. For instance, finding a sober New Year's Eve party can make all the difference in the world!

HOW MUCH AFTERCARE DOES MY TEENAGER NEED?

Addiction is a lifelong challenge, and no one can really predict the course of your teenager's recovery or the length and intensity of the aftercare treatment he should receive. Research on the outcome of addiction treatment consistently shows that substance users who stay in treatment longer have better outcomes—but that's a bit of a tautology: many patients who leave treatment sooner do so because they have relapsed. My advice as a clinician is that the young person in aftercare treatment remains connected for the longest possible time to professional treatment and, ideally, to peer-led support groups like AA.

A good example of the value of long-term aftercare is the experience of Diana, a seventeen-year-old woman who couldn't stop using cocaine on her own. Her parents insisted that she go through a twenty-one-day inpatient program, and she kicked her habit there. When she returned home, Diana went into an intensive outpatient program for eight weeks. She spent four evenings a week in group therapy and individual counseling, took daily drug tests, and went to an AA youth meeting on Saturdays. (Most of the kids in the meeting were in recovery from drug and alcohol problems.)

Although Diana didn't use any cocaine or other drugs during this period, she drank on a few occasions, which concerned her, her parents, and those of us trying to treat her. However, she was able to recommit to sobriety, and in eight weeks graduated from the IOP. Some of Diana's counselors weren't sure she was ready to leave, but her health insurance carrier would no longer pay for the program.

After Diana and her parents met with me a few times, we decided that she would continue coming to therapy once a week, have random drug tests in my office, attend AA meetings five times a week, and find a sponsor. Diana's commitment to sobriety seemed heartfelt to me, but she bristled at the idea of going to AA meetings so often and getting a sponsor. She made the excuses that her schoolwork would be quite heavy and that she needed time to reconnect with the friends whom she'd missed while in intensive treatment.

With my guidance, Diana's parents firmly told her that she had to attend AA meetings regularly for the time being. We all agreed, though, to be flexible as time went on. Diana somewhat reluctantly got a sponsor, who turned out to be exactly what she needed—a college junior who had struggled with cocaine and now had two years of sobriety under her belt. Her sponsor understood the pressures on Diana and was open-minded about how many meetings she should attend and how she could work the program's twelve steps. The adaptable and positive attitudes of her sponsor, parents, and me, made it easier for Diana to stay in treatment at the highest possible outpatient level.

The success of our approach to Diana's situation demonstrates how flexibility will work to the advantage of you and your recovering teenager as he goes through aftercare. As his life starts to come back together, he'll undoubtedly want to return to some, if not all, of his previous interests. This is a good thing, but the return to healthy activities must be balanced by a commitment to remain sober and to doing whatever is necessary to remain in control of his addiction. Your guidance, as well as that of the clinicians who will be treating your teenager, can be of great use to him.

Your teenager will inevitably take risks as he re-adapts to life, but you can help him manage and minimize them in a sensible way. For instance, even healthy relationships that don't involve substance use are fraught with emotional turmoil, especially for teenagers. Since building relationships is an integral part of growing up, you and your teenager have to discover how to build friendships that will help him stay away from drugs and alcohol. Many families insist that their teenagers be friends only with other sober teenagers, and they supervise those friendships as closely as possible.

PEER-LED SUPPORT GROUPS IN AFTERCARE

Recovering teenagers can make use of peer-led support groups such as AA in various ways. I always recommend that they maintain a strong, permanent connection to such groups, as this can protect them through high school, college, and beyond. You might need to negotiate with your teenager about her time commitment: her idea of how much is enough might not be the same as yours. As a rule of thumb, at the beginning of recovery, it's almost always a good idea to go to ninety meetings in ninety days and to connect with a sponsor. I've worked with teenagers who go to three or four meetings every day during their early recovery and benefit tremendously by doing so. Going to a lot of meetings makes it easier for your teenager to check in with a comfortable group rapidly when difficulties arise. Conversely, if a teenager who's newly in recovery starts dropping group meetings and friends, it can be a signal of impending relapse.

When your teenager's recovery has stabilized, however, the issue of balancing support-group involvement with the rest of her life often comes to the forefront. As her recovery progresses and she puts more and more distance between herself and her substance use, she might feel less and less need for peer-led support groups. Some of my patients go to a 12-step meeting every day, meet with their sponsor, and act as sponsors themselves, for decades. Others drop their programs entirely after establishing a few months of solid sobriety. (I don't recommend that!)

The majority of my teenage patients, when they feel secure in their recovery, simply cut down their group involvement so that it remains helpful, yet fits into the rest of their life. I treated one young man who, having benefited greatly from AA as he became sober, now attends a meeting once a month on a Saturday night, just to remind himself of what could happen to him. AA doesn't recommend this sort of intermittent or disengaged approach, but it can work for some teenagers. One perspective is that the AA phrase "take what you need, leave the rest" backs up the benefits of occasional attendance.

THE STEP-DOWN SYSTEM

So, you've gotten your teenager to inpatient treatment and he's completed the program. What next? Many recovering addicts know that the inpatient experience is easy when compared to life on the outside, which is full of stress, other people and, yes, drugs and alcohol. For your teenager, going from a good inpatient program to his old environment can be like going from zero to ninety miles an hour the instant he's discharged. He could suffer emotional whiplash. In fact, relapse is very common right after inpatient treatment ends. To ease the transition between inpatient treatment and the real world, many centers offer a "step-down program" of extended care after discharge. I unequivocally advocate step-down treatment. If your teenager's inpatient facility doesn't offer it, enlist his outside clinician's help in setting up a transitional plan for him in your own area.

Step-down might include enrollment in an intensive outpatient program attached to the inpatient facility. Your teenager would attend the program while living in a sober dorm or apartment before returning entirely to life at home, school, and work. Or he might enter a halfway house and live with other recovering addicts under a (widely varying) degree of supervision by licensed clinicians. After the halfway house phase, your teenager's program might offer him help in setting up sober living arrangements with other former patients. Together, the graduates sign a lease on a house or apartment, agree not to use drugs or alcohol, and agree to support each other in recovery. Some of the larger addiction treatment programs, such as Minnesota-based Hazelden, have a long, strong tradition of former patients helping and supporting each other in recovery. They set up roommate arrangements, find meetings, and even track down good jobs.

HALFWAY HOUSES

There are a lot of halfway houses out there, which isn't surprising given the considerable difficulties of becoming a fully functioning sober person. These aftercare facilities offer less treatment than inpatient rehabilitation, but provide a much more structured lifestyle than a private home does. They're often essential for teenagers who are just leaving inpatient programs, as it isn't easy to transition from the 24/7 treatment experience to life back at home—where conditions might not have changed at all. A halfway house can add tremendous value to your teenager's treatment by providing a relatively protected environment in which to try out relationships, work obligations, and school situations without the use of drugs and alcohol.

The degree of supervision that teenagers receive varies widely from halfway house to halfway house. Some are fully staffed, some rely on the residents to supervise and support each other, and some offer a combination of these scenarios. Of course, the quality of halfway houses also varies, and regulations can vary widely from state to state. If you're considering a halfway house for your teenager, look very carefully at the safety of the building itself, the skill and experience of any staff, and the general atmosphere.

For teenagers who need a high level of aftercare, the best approach is to bring them into a system of halfway houses and even less structured quarter-way houses that can provide as much or as little monitoring and support as they need. The next step after this is sometimes a sober house where recovering substance users agree to live together in a drug- and alcohol-free environment, with no supervision at all. These houses are ideal places to build a network of sober friends, find mentors, and track down practical advice about the sober lifestyle.

RESISTANCE TO AFTERCARE

Of course, just as with entering treatment in the first place, your teenager might be reluctant to undertake aftercare. A very common mode of resistance to treatment is the young person's wish to go back to being "normal"; that is, without an addiction problem, or at least free of the sometimes onerous requirements of addiction treatment.

Tough Talk Dialog: "I Don't Need All This Treatment Anymore."

Bobby:	Mrs. Jacobson, I can't get all this homework done. My parents still want me to go to my group once a week, go to AA three times a week, and go to see my therapist every week. I don't have any time for homework! You're a teacher— you know how much homework there is.
Mrs. Jacobson:	That's a lot! I imagine that you're busy every afternoon.
Bobby:	I am. It's weird—like I told you when I got home. I definitely get it this time. I can't drink or go back to my old friends. I know it—I don't need anyone to tell me about it. I'm not stupid— I would never go back. All this is way overkill.
Mrs. Jacobson:	Well, why do they say you have to do all this stuff?
Bobby:	My therapist said it's so I don't slip, but what does she know? Getting back to life and getting my grades up will keep me from slipping. I really want to do it this time.
Mrs. Jacobson:	I can see that, and I really respect you for that, Bobby. We all do and we're all pulling for you.
Bobby:	Can you talk to them? My parents, I mean? They're really pushing me to do all these require- ments. I don't need all this treatment anymore.
Mrs. Jacobson:	I will talk with them, but I don't think I should get into what kind of treatment you need. I'll leave that to the experts, but I can certainly help

> *you with managing your schoolwork. Really, Bobby, it's so cool that you're getting your life back together. You've done so well so far, maybe you should just stick with the plan. I'm sure the burdens on you will be less as time goes on.*

Bobby: *I guess so.*

Mrs. Jacobson: *They will. In the meantime, I can help you with your study planning so you can keep up with your classes.*

Bobby's teacher sympathizes with his sense of being snowed under, but she doesn't agree that he can drop treatment. Her understanding and offer of concrete help support his self-esteem and encourage him to stick with his aftercare. She focuses on what she knows—how to motivate a young person in his studies—by being an outstanding, caring teacher, and by leaving the treatment decisions to the clinicians. Although she probably agrees that Bobby should stay in the aftercare treatment plan recommended for him, she merely supports the professionals and Bobby's parents, rather than arguing the point herself. She "drives in her own lane."

DRUG AND ALCOHOL TESTING IN AFTERCARE

I strongly advocate testing teenagers in aftercare for drugs and alcohol, both "for cause" (when drug or alcohol use is suspected) and at random, to check the effectiveness of treatment. Those whose sobriety is strong might sometimes resent being tested, but most don't. Teenagers who are slipping back into substance use are prone to lying (duh!); testing reveals all. Many addicts say that knowing they'll be tested is a concrete reminder to stay away from drugs and alcohol. Even random testing can have this effect. A lot of my patients ask to be tested at random long after their aftercare plan requires it, simply as an added check on their slippery addictive thinking.

As with all drug and alcohol testing, the devil is in the details. Testing should be done, or at least managed, by a knowledgeable professional rather than by family members. This changes the testing's connotations from punitive ("you lied to me") to therapeutic ("we have a problem"). Sometimes, testing during aftercare can uncover a problem that your teenager doesn't even know is there by yielding an unexpected positive result.

Tough Talk Dialog: "No More Pills, but I Can Drink!"

Ramon: *So, Max, I asked you and your mom to come in before group today. You know, your urine from yesterday was positive for alcohol.*

Max: *What? You test for alcohol?*

Ramon: *Yeah—I'm your counselor, of course I do. Like I do for all substances of abuse.*

Carol: *What's going on, Max? I thought you were clean!*

Ramon: *Hold on, Mrs. B. I just want to let Max know about what we do, and then find out what's up. It's not a disaster, but we have to get to the bottom of this.*

Max: *OK, OK, I drank a few beers Tuesday night. It was no big deal.*

Ramon: *OK, that's it. I guess you weren't worried about relapsing to the OxyContin® again?*

Max: *No way! It was at Mark's party, there weren't any drugs around. Just me and a few other seniors playing poker for pennies.*

Carol: *They drink there? How could you?*

Ramon: *Hold up, hold up. I know this is upsetting, but we have to focus on the future here. What are your thoughts about drinking, Max?*

Max: *Well... I know you guys don't want me to drink, but it's really nothing. There's no way I could become an alcoholic. Or go back to the Oxy. That sucked! Look, I get it, I get it. No more pills, but I can drink!*

Ramon: *OK, you've identified the two main dangers to drinking—getting addicted to alcohol or slipping back to the Oxy. I know you decided to drink anyway, but I can see you've thought about it.*

Max: *Not really. You're telling me what you guys are worried about. I'm certainly not worried about either of those things happening to me!*

Ramon: *I can understand your not being worried, since it hasn't happened to you, but I've seen a lot of kids in your position say the same thing—and then have a lot of trouble with alcohol.*

Max: *Not me. It won't happen.*

Ramon: *Maybe not, but it's taking a big risk and if you don't like alcohol that much, there's no real reason for you to even try it. You know what it tastes like—you don't need to do any more research on that.*

Carol: *So why drink at all?*

Max: *You two make it sound so simple.*

Carol is understandably upset about her son's drinking, but Max's counselor Ramon models the most effective way to address his drinking: with concern, not panic.

RESPONDING TO SLIPS AND RELAPSES

So, your teenager has taken a drink or popped a pill again. Of course, you'd prefer that your teenager never pick up a drink or drug again. I do, too, but here on planet Earth addicts often relapse, and sometimes slip all the way back to needing inpatient treatment. Slips (brief incidents of substance use) and relapses (longer episodes) are unfortunately common in early sobriety.

If you discover that your teenager has slipped or relapsed, take a moment to gather your thoughts. How you respond to your teenager's setbacks is important: You don't want to freak out or exaggerate the severity of the situation. If your reaction is extreme, you'll overwhelm your teenager with your feelings, while if it's balanced, you'll be modeling the sort of response you want her to have to stressful situations. Frame your response so it's measured and sympathetic, but also realistic. You don't need to sugarcoat your feelings, ignore disaster signs, or back off from agreed-upon consequences.

Slips and relapses are certainly bad, but they're rarely catastrophes. The best reaction is concern and curiosity. How serious was the slip? Any idea what caused it? Most importantly, what can you take away from this one? It may be a bit much to ask that you respond with this sort of detached rationality if you discover that your teenager is again lying and using dangerous substances, but it's the best attitude to take, and it's the outlook that most therapists adopt.

I worked with one young woman who struggled to stop her use of alcohol, even (and especially) after she acknowledged to herself the self-destructive nature of the slips, which had cost her a number of friends, enormous amounts of money, and several jobs. After a second stint in rehab, she had a brief slip after work one day, when she stopped into a bar with some girlfriends and had two beers. Although she had not intended to drink or use cocaine, she found herself doing both. Her AA sponsor responded the next day with the timeworn adage, "Well, if you hang out in a barbershop, eventually you're going to get a haircut."

Although I and others had previously advised my patient to avoid bars, for some reason it was her sponsor's loving and succinct truth telling that got through to her. The simple aphorism helped her decide to steer clear of places that served alcohol. As her therapist, I could see that avoiding bars was eminently doable, while abstaining from alcohol *once she was in a bar* would be nearly impossible.

WHEN TO GO BACK TO INPATIENT TREATMENT

Increasing the intensity of your teenager's outpatient treatment might help him recover from a slip or relapse, but sometimes inpatient treatment is necessary. In determining if your teenager needs to go back into an inpatient facility, apply the same criteria that you did when you had him admitted the first time: If his addiction or psychiatric issues represent a serious danger, or if there's no other way that he can stop using, inpatient treatment is probably right for him. His addiction clinician has the experience to make this determination and to convince your teenager (and your insurance company) that he needs to be hospitalized again. Often, a second round of inpatient can function as a quick "booster" and need not last as long as the initial treatment.

A return to inpatient treatment isn't a failure (on anyone's part!). In fact, it's usually a success story of sorts. Rather than simply suffering with his addiction, your teenager (or you, or his teachers, or his friends) realized that he has a problem, he knows where to go for help, and he has successfully acted on that knowledge. Reentering inpatient treatment is one not-so-small step forward for your teenager—and you!

This is my message of hope for you and your teenager. Although addiction is a chronic, lifelong problem, it can be relegated to a very small corner of your teenager's life. One of the great pleasures of working with addicted teenagers is witnessing them conquer seemingly insurmountable challenges—even if it takes a few attempts. There's nothing more rewarding than watching addicted teenagers change and grow and eventually reach the sobriety that they set out to achieve. Their addiction never quite leaves them, but it morphs into something less overpowering: a vulnerability to addictive behavior. Your teenager must remain vigilant for the rest of his life, but his addiction doesn't have to hold him back from anything!

POINTS TO REMEMBER

- The best aftercare makes a direct connection between intensive outpatient or inpatient treatment and your teenager's return to normal life.
- Peer-led support groups such as AA are enormously helpful to recovering teenagers.
- Keep having your teenager tested for drugs and alcohol.
- Respond calmly to slips and relapses.
- Vulnerability to addiction is lifelong, but need not hold your teenager back!

SECTION IV:

APPENDICES

Appendix A

GLOSSARY OF SELECTED DRUG TERMINOLOGY AND SLANG

O ver the years, I've learned a lot of addiction-related slang from my patients and the Internet. Here's a list of common words and phrases that you might hear from your substance-using teenager or his friends. I have also included a few slang terms related to eating disorders, gambling, and sex addiction. You can also find up-to-date lists of drug lingo on the website of the Office of National Drug Control Policy: www.streetlightpublications.net/misc/ondcp. htm or on the drugs page of the private slang site, www.noslang. com/drugs/dictionary.php.

▶A

Abandominiums: Abandoned row houses where drugs are used
Abe: $5.00 worth of drugs
A-Bomb: Marijuana cigarette laced with heroin or opium
AC/DC: Codeine cough syrup
Acapulco Gold: Marijuana from southwest Mexico
Acapulco Red: Marijuana
Acid: LSD
Acid Head: User of LSD
Adam: MDMA
Air Blast: Inhalants

Airplane: Marijuana
Al Capone: Heroin
All-Star: User of multiple drugs
All-American drug: Cocaine
Amoeba: PCP
Amp Joint: Marijuana cigarette laced with some form of narcotic
Amped: High on amphetamines
Amped-Out: Fatigued after using amphetamine
Amping: Accelerated heartbeat
Ana: A person with anorexia nervosa
Angel Dust: PCP
Angel Hair: PCP
Angel Mist: PCP
Angel Poke: PCP
Animal Trank: PCP
Arnolds: Anabolic steroids
Aspirin: Cocaine
Astro Turf: Marijuana
Atom Bomb: Marijuana mixed with heroin
Aunt Hazel: Heroin
Aunt Mary: Marijuana
Author: Doctor who writes illegal prescriptions

▶ B
Baby: Cocaine; marijuana
Babysitter: Marijuana
Backwards: Depressants
Badrock: Crack cocaine
Bagging: Using inhalants
Baked: High on marijuana
Bams: Amphetamine; depressants
Bamba: Marijuana
Bar: Large quantity of cannabis; one-ounce bar or one-kilogram bar
Barbs: Barbiturates
Bart Simpson: Heroin

Baryphobia: Anxiety-driven fear of becoming obese
Base: Freebase cocaine; to use freebase cocaine
Base Head: Person who bases
Baseball: Crack cocaine
Bash: Marijuana
Bathtub Crank: Poor quality methamphetamine
Batman: Cocaine; heroin; mixture of cocaine and heroin
Battery Acid: LSD
Bazooka: Cocaine; combination of crack cocaine and marijuana;
    crack and tobacco combined in a cigarette; coca (cocaine)
    paste and marijuana
B-Bombs: Amphetamine; MDMA
Beamer: Crack smoker
Bean: Capsule containing drugs; MDMA
Beannies: Methamphetamine
Beast: Heroin plus LSD
Beavis & Butthead: LSD
Beemers: Crack cocaine
Bender: Drug party
Bennies: Amphetamine
Benzos: Benzodiazepines; tranquilizers
Bernice: Cocaine
B-40: Cigar laced with marijuana and dipped in malt liquor
Big C: Cocaine
Bigflake: Cocaine
Big O: Opium
Bin Laden: Heroin
Birdie Powder: Cocaine; heroin
Biscuit: $50 rocks of crack
BJs: Crack cocaine
Black Beauties: Amphetamine; depressants
Black Eagle: Heroin
Black Hash: Opium mixed with hashish
Black Mollies: Amphetamine
Black Pearl: Heroin

Black Russian: Opium mixed with hashish
Black Tar: Heroin
Black Whack: PCP
Blanket: Marijuana cigarette
Blaze a Roach: To smoke marijuana
Blast a Stick: To smoke marijuana
Blizzard: White cloud in a pipe used to smoke cocaine
Blonde: Marijuana
Blotter: Small paper square saturated with dissolved LSD; crack
    cocaine
Blow: Cocaine; to snort cocaine; to smoke marijuana; to inject heroin
Blow Smoke: To snort cocaine
Blow Up: Crack cut with the anesthetic lidocaine to increase the
    drug's volume, weight, and street value
Blowcaine: Crack diluted with the anesthetic procaine
Blowing Smoke: Marijuana
Blowout: Crack cocaine
Blows: Heroin
Blue: Crack cocaine; depressants; OxyContin®
Blue Boys: Amphetamine
Blue Chairs: LSD
Blue Devils: Methamphetamine
Blue Kisses: MDMA
Blue Microdot: LSD
Blue Star: Heroin
Blunt: Cigar containing marijuana; cigar containing cocaine and
    marijuana
Bob Hope: Marijuana; cannabis
Bogart a Joint: To salivate on a marijuana cigarette; refuse to share it
Bone: Marijuana; $50 piece of crack; high-purity heroin
Bones: Crack cocaine
Boo: Marijuana; methamphetamine
Booda: Large, strong marijuana cigarette, sometimes with crack
Booster: To snort cocaine
Bopper: Crack cocaine

Boulder: Crack cocaine; $20 worth of crack
Boulya: Crack cocaine
Brain Damage: Heroin
Brain Ticklers: Amphetamine
Brick: Crack cocaine; cocaine; marijuana; one kilogram of
  marijuana
Broccoli: Marijuana
Brown Sugar: Heroin
Brownies: Amphetamine
Bud: Marijuana
Buda: Marijuana; a high-grade marijuana joint filled with crack
Buddha: Potent marijuana spiked with opium
Buddha: Large, strong marijuana cigarette, sometimes with crack
Bugged: Irritated; to be covered with sores and abscesses from
  repeated use of non-sterile needles
Bullyon: Marijuana
Bump: Crack; fake crack; cocaine; boost a high; $20 worth of
  ketamine
Burn One: To smoke marijuana
Burn the Main Line: To inject a drug
Burnout: Heavy abuser of drugs
Bush: Marijuana; cocaine; PCP
Butane: Cigarette lighter gas used as an inhalant
Buzz: Under the influence of drugs

▶ C
C Joint: Place where cocaine is sold
Cabbage Head: Person who will use or experiment with any kind
  of drug
Cafeteria use: Use of various drugs simultaneously, particularly
  sedatives or hypnotics
Cafeteria-style use: Using a combination of different club drugs
Callies: Type of MDMA
Came: Cocaine
Candy: Cocaine; crack cocaine; amphetamine; depressants

Candy Raver: People who attend raves; ravers who wear jewelry made of candy

Candyman: Drug supplier

Cannabis Tea: Marijuana

Cap: Crack cocaine; LSD; a capsule of a drug

Captain Cody: Codeine

Carburetor: Crack stem attachment

Casper: Crack cocaine

Casper the Ghost: Crack cocaine

Catnip: Marijuana cigarette

Chalking: Chemically altering the color of cocaine so it looks white

Charley: Heroin

Charlie: Cocaine

Chaser: Compulsive crack user

Chasing the Dragon: Using a tube to inhale the curl of smoke from heroin heated on a piece of aluminum foil; crack mixed with heroin

Cherry Meth: GHB

Chicago Green: Marijuana

Chicken Scratch: Searching on hands and knees for crack or cocaine that's been dropped

Chieva: Heroin

China Girl: Fentanyl

Chinatown: Fentanyl

China White: Heroin plus fentanyl; synthetic heroin

Chipping: Using drugs occasionally

Chocolate: Marijuana; opium amphetamine

Chocolate Chips: LSD

Christmas Bud: Marijuana

Chunky: Marijuana

Cinnamon: Methamphetamine

Clear: Methamphetamine

Climb: Marijuana cigarette

Cloud: Crack cocaine

Coca: Cocaine

Cocaine Blues: Depression after extended cocaine use

Coco Snow: The anesthetic benzocaine used as a cutting agent for crack

Cocoa Puff: To smoke cocaine and marijuana

Coke: Cocaine

Coke Bar: Bar where cocaine is openly used

Cokehead: Cocaine user

Cold Turkey: Symptoms and experience of withdrawing from heroin, including goose bumps

Columbian: Marijuana

Colorado Cocktail: Marijuana

Connect: To purchase drugs; supplier of illegal drugs

Cooker: To inject a drug; person who manufactures methamphetamine

Cookies: Crack cocaine

Coolie: Cigarette laced with cocaine

Cooking-Up: Preparing drugs, especially heroin, for injection

Cop: To obtain drugs

Copping zones: Specific areas where buyers can purchase drugs

Corn: Marijuana

Cottaging (British): Anonymous sex between men, in a bathroom

Cotton: Money; OxyContin®

Courage Pills: Heroin; depressants

Cousin Tina: Crystal meth

Crack: Cocaine that has been treated so it can be smoked

Crack Bash: Combination of crack cocaine and marijuana

Crack Gallery: Place where crack cocaine is bought and sold

Crack in the Box: Busy gas station where drug transactions often take place

Crash: To sleep off the effects of drugs

Crazy Eddie: PCP

Crazy Weed: Marijuana

Cripple: Marijuana cigarette

Crisscross: Amphetamine

Cron: Marijuana

Cronic: Marijuana
Crystal Joint: PCP
Crystal Meth: Methamphetamine
Cube: LSD, one ounce
Cupcakes: LSD
Cut: Adulterants added to a drug, especially cocaine, to increase
    its bulk; to add adulterants to a drug
Cut Deck: Heroin mixed with powdered milk

▶D
Date-Rape drug: Rohypnol®
Dawamesk: Marijuana
Dead on Arrival: Heroin
Dead President: Heroin
Deisel: Heroin
Demolish: Crack
Dep-Testosterone: Injectable anabolic steroid
Detroit Pink: PCP
Devil, the: Crack cocaine
Devil Drug: Crack cocaine
Devil's Bush: Marijuana
Devil's Dandruff: Cocaine
Devil's Dick: Crack pipe
Devil's Dust: PCP
Dew: Marijuana
Dexies: Amphetamine-containing stimulants such as Dexedrine
    and dexamphetamine sulphate
Dianabol: Veterinary anabolic steroid; veterinary
    and oral
Dice: Crack cocaine
Diesel: Heroin
Diet Pills: Amphetamine
Dime: $10 worth of marijuana
Dime Bag: $10 bag of drugs
Dinosaurs: Populations of heroin users in their forties and fifties

Dipped Joints: Cigarettes containing marijuana combined with PCP and the embalming fluid formaldehyde

Dipper: PCP

Dipping Out: Crack runners (people who transport drugs for dealers) stealing a portion of crack from the vials

Dips: Marijuana cigarettes dipped in PCP

Dirt: Heroin

Disco Biscuits: Depressants; MDMA

Disease: Drug of choice

Djamba: Marijuana

Doctor Shopping: Going from doctor to doctor to get multiple prescriptions

Don Juan: Marijuana

Donkey: Ketamine

Doobie: Marijuana cigarette

Dope: Cannabis; heroin

Dope Smoke: To smoke marijuana

Dose: LSD

Dots: LSD

Double-Breasted Dealing: Dealing cocaine and heroin together

Double Rock: Crack double diluted with the anesthetic procaine

Double-Up: To throw in a free rock of crack with the purchase of another, as a ploy to attract customers

Down: Codeine cough syrup

Downers: Depressant drugs

Dr. Feel Good: Heroin

Dream: Cocaine

Dreamer: Morphine

Drop: To take or swallow a drug

Dry High: Marijuana

Dummy Dust: PCP

Dust: Marijuana mixed with various chemicals; cocaine; heroin; PCP

Dust Joint: PCP

Dynamite: Cocaine mixed with heroin

▶E

E: Ecstasy (MDMA)
Earth: Marijuana cigarette
Easy Lay: GHB
E-bombs: Ecstasy (MDMA)
Ecstasy: MDMA
Egyptians: MDMA
Eightball: One-eighth of an ounce of drugs; crack cocaine mixed
    with heroin
Eighth: One-eighth of an ounce of cannabis
El Gallo ("rooster"): Marijuana
El Perico ("parrot"): Cocaine
Electric Kool-Aid: LSD
Elephant Flipping: Using PCP and MDMA
Embalming Fluid: PCP
E-Puddle: Sleeping off exhaustion due to MDMA use
Equipoise: Veterinary anabolic steroid
E-Tard: Person under the influence of MDMA
Eve: MDMA
Ever Clear: Cocaine; GHB
Ex: Ecstasy (MDMA)

▶F

Face: Cocaine
Fantasy: GHB
Fast: Amphetamines; crack cocaine; methamphetamine
Fat Bags: Crack cocaine
Fatty: Marijuana cigarette
Fir: Marijuana
Fire it up: To smoke marijuana
First Line: Morphine
Five-Way, the: Blend of heroin plus cocaine plus methamphetamine
    plus Rohypnol® plus alcohol
Fives: Amphetamine
Flakka: An amphetamine-like stimulant

Flame Cooking: Smoking cocaine base by putting the pipe over a stove flame

Flamethrower: Cigarette laced with cocaine and heroin

Flashback: Moment of an LSD trip that's reexperienced long after the original trip

Flasher: Exhibitionist

Flat Chunks: Crack cut with the anesthetic benzocaine

Flea Powder: Low-purity heroin

Flipping: Using MDMA

Florida Snow: Cocaine

Flower: Marijuana

Flower Flipping: Using MDMA mixed with hallucinogenic mushrooms

Flying: Under the influence of drugs

Foil: Heroin

Foo Foo Dust: Cocaine

Foolish Powder: Cocaine; heroin

Footballs: Amphetamine

Forget-Me Drug: Rohypnol®

Freebase: Cocaine that has been treated so it can be smoked

French Fries: Crack cocaine

Fresh: PCP

Friend: Fetanyl

Fry: Marijuana cigarette dipped in embalming fluid, sometimes also laced with PCP; marijuana cigarette laced with PCP

Fuel: Marijuana mixed with insecticides

▶ G

Galloping Horse: Heroin

Gallup: Heroin

Gamma Oh: GHB

Gangster Pills: Depressants

Ganja: Marijuana; cannabis

Garbage Head: User of multiple drugs

Garbage Rock: Crack cocaine

Gas: Butane gas, a volatile substance, used as inhalant
Gash: Marijuana
Gauge Butt: Marijuana
GB: Depressants
Gear: Drugs
Geek Joints: Cigarettes or cigars laced with crack cocaine;
    marijuana cigarettes laced with cocaine or crack cocaine
Georgia Home Boy: GHB
Get Lifted: To get high or intoxicated
Getgo: Methamphetamine
Getting Glassed: To snort methamphetamine
Getting Roached: Using Rohypnol®
Getting Snotty: Using heroin
Ghana: Marijuana
GHB: The depressant gamma-Hydroxybutyric acid
Ghost, the: LSD
Gift of the Sun: Cocaine
Giggle Weed: Marijuana
Girlfriend: Cocaine
Glad Stuff: Cocaine
Glue: Adhesives that are inhaled to produce a high
Goat: Heroin
God's Medicine: Opium
Go-Fast: Methamphetamine
Gold Dust: Cocaine
Gold Star: Marijuana
Golden Girl: Heroin
Golf Balls: Depressants
Good and Plenty: Heroin
Good Butt: Marijuana cigarette
Good H: Heroin
Goodfellas: Fentanyl
Goon Dust: PCP
Gorge: Marijuana
Gorilla Pills: Depressants

Graduate: Completely stop using drugs; progress to stronger drugs
Grass: Cannabis, in herbal form
Grass Brownies: Marijuana
Grasshopper: Marijuana
Gravel: Crack cocaine
Great Bear: Fentanyl
Greek: Combination of marijuana and cocaine
Green: Herbal cannabis; marijuana
Green Frog: Depressants
Green Goddess: Marijuana
Greenies: Amphetamines; MDMA
Greens: Marijuana
Greta: Marijuana
Grievous Bodily Harm: GHB
Grit: Crack cocaine
Grizzy: Marijuana
G-Rock: One gram of crack cocaine
Gum: Opium; MDMA
Gym Candy: Anabolic steroids

▶ H
Hache: Heroin
Haircut: Marijuana
Hairy: Heroin
Half Moon: Peyote
Happy Powder: Cocaine
Happy Stick: Marijuana and PCP combination
Hard Ball: Crack cocaine
Hardware: Poppers; inhalants
Harry: Heroin
Harsh: Marijuana
Hash: Cannabis resin
Have a Dust: To take cocaine
Hawaiian: Very high-potency marijuana
Hawaiian Black: Marijuana

Hay: Marijuana

H-bomb: MDMA mixed with heroin

H-Caps: Heroin

Heat: Police or narcotics officers

Heavenly Blue: LSD

Heeled: Having plenty of money

Hell: Crack cocaine

Hemp: Non-marijuana variety of cannabis plant valued for its oil-rich seeds and for the fiber in its stalk, used to make fabric and rope

Henry: One-eighth of an ounce of marijuana

Herb: Marijuana

Herbal Bliss: MDMA

Hit: Dose of drugs; a drug injection; the effect of drugs reaching the brain

Hit House: Where users go to shoot up and pay the owner in drugs

Hit the Hay: To smoke marijuana

Hitter: Small pipe designed for smoking only one hit

Homegrown: Marijuana, typically of low potency, picked from herbal cannabis plants grown on a small scale, often in users' homes

Homicide: Heroin cut with the hallucinogen scopolamine or the poison strychnine

Hooch: Marijuana, also alcohol

Hooked: Addicted to or dependent on drugs

Horn: To snort a drug, especially cocaine; crack pipe

Horse: Heroin

Horse Heads: Amphetamines

Horse Tracks: PCP

Hot Dope: Heroin

Hot Rolling: Liquefying methamphetamine in an eye dropper and then inhaling it

Hotrailing: To heat methamphetamine and inhale the vapor through the nose using a plastic tube

Huff: Inhalants

Huffer: Inhalant abuser

Huffing: To inhale an inhalant
Hype: Heroin addict; an addict; MDMA

▶ I

I am Back: Crack cocaine
Ice: Methamphetamine; powerful smokable stimulant
Ice Cream Habit: Occasional use of drugs
Idiot Pills: Depressants
Illies: Marijuana dipped in PCP
Illing: Marijuana dipped in PCP
Illy: Marijuana cigarette soaked in embalming fluid and dried
Inca Message: Cocaine
Indian Hay: Marijuana from India
Indonesian Bud: Marijuana; opium
Instant Zen: LSD
Interplanetary Mission: Travel from one crack house to another to
    search for crack cocaine

▶ J

J: Marijuana cigarette
Jab: To inject a drug
Jacking up: Injecting a drug
Jackson: Amphetamine
Jane: Marijuana
Jay: Marijuana cigarette
Jay Smoke: Marijuana
Jenny: Heroin
Jerry Garcias: MDMA
Jive Stick: Marijuana
Joint: Marijuana cigarette
Jolly Beans: Amphetamine
Jolly Green: Marijuana
Jones: To be in need of drugs; to crave drugs
Joy: Heroin
Joy popping: Occasional use of drugs

Joy Powder: Cocaine; heroin
Jugs: Amphetamine
Juice: PCP; anabolic steroids
Juja: Marijuana
Junco: Heroin
Junk: Cocaine; heroin
Junkie: Drug addict, especially a heroin addict
Junkie Kits: Glass pipe and copper mesh

K

K: PCP
K Blast: PCP
K-Hole: Periods of ketamine-induced confusion; the depressant
    high associated with ketamine
K-Holing: Taking ketamine; the experience of using ketamine
Kabuki: Crack pipe made from a plastic rum bottle and a rubber
    spark plug cover
Kentucky Blue: Marijuana
Khat: Amphetamine; methcathinone (a stimulant similar to
    methamphetamine); MDMA
Kicker: OxyContin®
Kiddie Dope: Prescription drugs
Killer Green Bud: Marijuana
Killer Weed: Marijuana
King: Cocaine
King Bud: Marijuana
Kools: PCP
Krippy: Marijuana
Krokodil: Desomorphine
Kryptonite: Crack cocaine; marijuana
Kush: Marijuana

▶L

L: LSD
Lady Caine: Cocaine

Lady Snow: Cocaine
Lan: Poker addict, usually of Asian descent
Late Night: Cocaine
Laughing Gas: Nitrous oxide, a gas that produces euphoric effects
  when inhaled
Laughing Grass: Marijuana
Laughing Weed: Marijuana
Lazy Bitch: One pound of marijuana
Lemonade: Heroin; poor-quality drugs
Lethal Weapon: PCP
Lettuce: Money
Lick the Bones: To smoke crack cocaine
Lid Poppers: Amphetamine
Lid Proppers: Amphetamine
Lime Acid: LSD
Lipton Tea: Poor-quality drugs
Liquid G: GHB
Lit: Under the influence of drugs
Lit Up: Under the influence of drugs
Little Boy: Heroin
Little Ones: PCP
Live Ones: PCP
Llesca: Marijuana
Locker Room: Isobutyl nitrite; inhalants
Loco ("crazy"): Marijuana
Loco Weed: Marijuana
Loony Tunes: LSD
Love: Crack cocaine
Love Drug: Depressants; MDMA
LSD: The hallucinogen lysergic acid
  diethylamide
Lucy: LSD
Lucy in the Sky with Diamonds: LSD
Ludes: Depressants; Quaaludes (methaqualone)
Lunch Money Drug: Rohypnol®

▶M

Macaroni and Cheese: $5.00 bag of marijuana plus a $10 bag of
    cocaine
Mafu (Spanish): Marijuana
Magic Mushrooms: Hallucinogenic mushrooms
Mainline: To inject a drug
Mainlining: Using drugs intravenously
Mama Coca: Cocaine
Mani-Wowie: Marijuana; methamphetamine
Mania Coca: Cocaine
Manteca: Heroin
Marathons: Amphetamines
Marching Dust: Cocaine
Marijonas: Marijuana
Marshmallow Reds: Depressants
Mary: Marijuana
Mary and Johnny: Marijuana
Maryann: Marijuana
Maryjane: Marijuana
Marywarner: Marijuana
Mary Weaver: Marijuana
Maserati: Crack pipe made from a plastic rum bottle and a rubber
    spark plug cover
Maui-Wowie: Marijuana; methamphetamine
Mayo: Cocaine; heroin
MDA: The hallucinogen methylenedioxyamphetamine
MDMA: The hallucinogen methylenedioxymethamphetamine
Mesc: Mescaline, the hallucinogenic drug found in peyote
Meth: Methamphetamine; methadone
Mexican Horse: Heroin
Mexican Mud: Heroin
Mia: A person with bulimia
MiAna: A person with anorexia and bulimia
Mickey Finn: Depressants, also Rohypnol® or scopolamine
Microdots: LSD in pellets a little larger than two millimeters in
    diameter

Mighty Quinn: LSD

Mighty White: A form of crack cocaine that is hard, white, and pure

Miss: To inject a drug

Miss Emma: Morphine

Mister Blue: Morphine

MJ: Marijuana

MO: Marijuana; cocaine

Mojo: Cocaine; heroin

Molly: MDMA, usually the powder form

Money Talks: Heroin

Monkey Dust: PCP

Monster: Cocaine

Moon Gas: Inhalants

Moota: Marijuana

Morning Shot: Amphetamine; MDMA

Mortal Combat: High-potency heroin

Mother's Little Helper: Depressants

Movie Star Drug: Cocaine

Mow the Grass: To smoke marijuana

Muggle: Marijuana

Mule: Person who transports drugs for dealers

Mushrooms: Mushrooms containing the hallucinogen psilocybin or psilocin

Murder 8: Fentanyl

Mutah: Marijuana

Mutha: Marijuana

▶N

Nice and Easy: Heroin

Nickelonians: Crack addicts

Nick: Five dollars

Nigra: Marijuana

No Worries: Depressant

Nod: Effects of heroin

Nose Candy: Cocaine

Nose Drops: Liquefied heroin
Nose Stuff: Cocaine
Nox: Use of nitrous oxide (a gas that produces euphoric effects when inhaled) and MDMA
Number: Marijuana cigarette

▶O

Oatmeal: Marijuana
OC: OxyContin®
OD: Overdose
Off: Drug-free (e.g., "I'm off the gear now.")
Oil: Cannabis oil, an oily liquid high in THC; heroin; PCP
Old Navy: Heroin
On a Trip: Under the influence of drugs
On Ice: In jail
On the Ball: To shave a slice of MDMA into a bag of heroin
On the Bricks: Walking the streets
On the Nod: Under the influence of narcotics or depressants
One and One: To snort cocaine
One-on-One House: Where cocaine and heroin can be purchased
Onion: Ounce
Oolies: Marijuana cigarettes laced with crack cocaine
Ope: Opium
Optical Illusions: LSD
Orange Barrels: LSD
Orange Crystal: PCP
Orange Haze: LSD
Orange Line: Heroin
Os: OxyContin®
Ox: OxyContin®
Oxicotten: Semisynthetic opioid
Oxies: Oxycodone
Oxy: OxyContin®
Oxy 80: Semisynthetic opioid
Oxycet: Semisynthetic opioid

Oxycotton: OxyContin®
Oxys: Oxycodone
Oyster Stew: Cocaine
Oz: Inhalants
Ozone: Marijuana, PCP and crack cigarette; marijuana cigarette; PCP

▶P
Pack of Rocks: Marijuana cigarette
Pakalolo: Marijuana
Pakistani Black: Marijuana
Pancakes and Syrup: Combination of the hypnotic sedative glutethimide and codeine cough syrup
Panic: Drugs not available
Paper: Dose of heroin; one-tenth of a gram or less of methamphetamine
Paper Boy: Heroin peddler
Parabolin: Veterinary anabolic steroid taken orally
Parachute Down: Using MDMA after heroin
Paradise White: Cocaine
Pariba: Cocaine
Party and Play: Methamphetamine used in combination with MDMA and the erectile dysfunction medication Viagra®
Paste: Crack cocaine
PCP: The hallucinogen phencyclidine
P-Dogs: Combination of cocaine and marijuana
Peace Tablets: LSD
Pee Wee: Crack cocaine; $5.00 worth of crack cocaine
Peeping Tom: Voyeur
Peg: Heroin
Pellets: LSD
Pen Ya Peruvian: Opium
Penyan: Opium
Penguins: LSD blotters illustrated with a picture of a penguin
Pep Pills: Amphetamine

Perc-a-Pop: Berry-flavored lozenge on a stick, containing fentanyl

Perp: Fake crack cocaine made of candle wax and baking soda

Peruvian: Cocaine

Peruvian Flake: Cocaine

Peyote: Type of cactus that contains the hallucinogen mescaline

Pharming: Simultaneously consuming an assortment of prescription medications

Phillies Blunt: Cigar filled with marijuana

Piedra (Spanish): Crack cocaine

Piff: Marijuana

Pig Killer: PCP

Pikachu: Pills containing PCP and MDMA

Pill House: Residence where pills are sold illicitly

Pills: Drugs in pill form; MDMA; OxyContin®

Pimp: Cocaine

Pink Elephants: Methamphetamine

Pink Panthers: MDMA

Pinned: Under the influence of opioids

Pixies: Amphetamine

Point: Needle

Poison: Heroin; fentanyl

Pokeritis: Addiction to playing poker, either online or live

Pony: Crack cocaine

Poor Man's Coke: Methamphetamine

Pop: To snort cocaine; crack cocaine

Poppers: Isobutyl nitrate or amyl nitrate, which reduce blood pressure; methamphetamine

Poppy: Heroin

Pot: Cannabis; marijuana

Powder Diamonds: Cocaine

Predator: Heroin

Pregorexia: Condition in which a pregnant woman restricts calories to avoid weight gain

Press: Cocaine; crack cocaine

Primo: Crack cocaine; marijuana mixed with cocaine; crack and heroin; heroin; cocaine and tobacco

Primos: Cigarettes laced with cocaine and heroin
Pro-Ana: Person or organization who supports anorexia as a
    reasonable lifestyle choice
Psychedelic: Hallucinogenic
Puff: Cannabis; marijuana
Puff the Dragon: To smoke marijuana
Puffer: Crack cocaine smoker
Pumpers: Anabolic steroids
Purple Caps: Crack cocaine
Purple Pills: MDMA
Push Shorts: To cheat a drug buyer by selling short amounts
Pyramiding: Strategy for use of anabolic steroids

▶ Q

Qat: Khat; amphetamine; methcathinone (a stimulant similar to
    methamphetamine); MDMA
QP: One-quarter pound of marijuana
Quartz: Smokable methamphetamine
Queen Anne's Lace: Marijuana
Quicksilver: Poppers; inhalants

▶ R

Racehorse Charlie: Cocaine; heroin
Rainy Day Woman: Marijuana
Rave: All-night dance parties where music and lights are frequently
    used to enhance the effects of hallucinogenic drugs
Rawhide: Heroin
R-Ball: Ritalin®
Recompress: Change the shape of cocaine flakes to resemble rock
    cocaine
Recycle: LSD
Red Devils: MDMA
Red Lips: LSD
Redneck Cocaine: Methamphetmine
Reds: Depressants
Reefer: Marijuana

Reindeer Dust: Heroin

Res: Potent residue left in the pipe after crack cocaine is smoked—
it's scraped out and smoked

Rest in Peace: Crack cocaine

Rhine: Heroin

Rhubarb and Custard: Type of MDMA, usually sold in yellow and
purple capsules

Richard: Cocaine

Rig: Equipment used to inject drugs

Righteous Bush: Marijuana

Roach: Butt of a marijuana cigarette; small piece of cardboard
placed in the end of a large marijuana cigarette

Roach Clip: Clip used to hold a partially smoked marijuana cigarette

Roasting: Smoking marijuana

Roche: Rohypnol®

Rock: Crack cocaine

Rock Attack: Crack cocaine

Rock Star: Female who trades sex for crack or money to buy crack;
a person who uses rock cocaine

Rocket Fuel: PCP

Rocks: Lumps of crack cocaine

Rocks of Hell: Crack cocaine

Rocky: Cannabis resin, usually hard and with a dry texture
(hashish, hash)

Rocky III: Crack cocaine

Roid Rage: Aggressive behavior caused by excessive anabolic
steroid use

Rollin': High on MDMA

Roofies: Rohypnol®

Rough Stuff: Marijuana

Ruffies: Rohypnol®

Rugs: Marijuana

Runner: A person who transports drugs for a dealer

Rush: Cocaine; poppers; inhalants

Rush Hour: Heroin

▶S

Sack: Heroin

Sacrament: LSD

Salt and Pepper: Marijuana

Salty Water: GHB

Sativa: Species of cannabis, found in cool damp climates

Scag: Heroin

Scarecrow: OxyContin®; Lortab® (acetaminophen and hydrocodone)

Schwagg: Marijuana

Score: To purchase drugs illegally

Scrape and Snort: To share crack cocaine by scraping small pieces off a rock for snorting

Script: Prescription, usually for controlled drugs

Scruples: Crack cocaine

Second to None: Heroin

Sen: Marijuana

Sensimellia: Cannabis; flowering heads of the female cannabis plant

Sextasy: Ecstasy used with Viagra®

Shake: Marijuana mixed with cocaine

Sherm: Hallucinogenic mushrooms; PCP

Sherm: Tobacco laced with PCP

Sherman Stick: Crack cocaine; PCP; cigars dipped in or laced with PCP

Shermhead: Crackhead

Shit: Heroin; cannabis

Shmeck: Heroin

Shoot: Heroin

Shoot the Breeze: Nitrous oxide, a gas that produces euphoric effects when inhaled

Shot to the Curb: One who has lost it all to crack

Shrooms: Hallucinogenic mushrooms

Silver Bullet: Ritalin®

Sixteenth: One-sixteenth of an ounce of cannabis

Skag: Heroin

Skee: Opium
Skid: Heroin
Skied: Under the influence of drugs
Skin Popping: Injecting drugs under the skin on any part of the
    body, without hitting a vein
Skittles: Coricidin®, a cough and cold remedy that acts as a
    hallucinogen in high doses
Skittling: Abusing Coricidin®
Skunk: Marijuana; heroin
Skunkweed: Marijuana
Slamming: Amphetamine; MDMA
Sleeper: Heroin; depressants
Smack: Heroin
Smoke: Marijuana; crack cocaine; heroin and crack
Smoke a bowl: To smoke marijuana
Smokehouse: Residence where crack cocaine is smoked
Smoke-Out: Under the influence of drugs
Smoking: PCP
Smoking Gun: Heroin and cocaine
Smooch: Crack cocaine
Smurf: Cigar dipped in embalming fluid
Smurfs: MDMA
Snap: Amphetamine
Sniff: Cocaine
Snop: Marijuana
Snort: To take drugs, mainly cocaine, amphetamines, or heroin, by
    inhaling them into the nose.
Snotballs: Rubber cement rolled into balls and burned so the
    fumes can be inhaled
Snow: Cocaine
Snow Pallets: Amphetamine
Snowball: Ecstasy-type drug containing MDMA and MDA
Snowcones: Cocaine
Soap: Cannabis resin, usually in the form of smooth, brown,
    rounded bars; GHB; crack cocaine; methamphetamine

Soap Dope: Methamphetamine with a pinkish tint
Society High: Cocaine
Solid: Cannabis resin
South Parks: LSD
Space: Crack cocaine
Space Cadet: Crack dipped in PCP
Space Dust: Crack dipped in PCP
Space Ship: Glass pipe used to smoke crack cocaine
Space Ball: PCP used with cocaine or crack cocaine
Special K: Ketamine
Speed: Amphetamines; crack cocaine; methamphetamine
Speedball: Mixture of a stimulant and a depressant, usually speed
    plus heroin, or cocaine plus heroin; crack cocaine mixed with
    cocaine; Ritalin® mixed with heroin; amphetamine
Speedball: To shoot up or smoke a mixture of cocaine and heroin;
    MDMA mixed with ketamine; to smoke or shoot up a
    speedball
Spider: Heroin
Splash: Amphetamine
Spliff: Cannabis; cannabis mixed with tobacco; large marijuana
    cigarette
Splim: Marijuana
Split: Adulterated drugs
Splitting: Rolling marijuana and cocaine into a cigarette together
Spoosh: Methamphetamine
Sporting: Snorting cocaine
Stack: Marijuana
Stackers: Anabolic steroids
Stacking: MDMA adulterated with heroin or crack; protocol for
    using anabolic steroids
Stamp: LSD
Stardust: Cocaine; PCP
Step-On: To dilute drugs
Sticky Icky: Marijuana
Stoned: Under the influence of drugs, especially cannabis

Stones: Lumps of crack cocaine
Straw: Marijuana cigarette
Strawberry Fields: LSD
Studio Fuel: Cocaine
Sugar: Cocaine; crack cocaine; heroin; LSD
Sugar Block: Crack cocaine
Sugar Boogers: Cocaine
Sugar Cubes: LSD
Sugar Lumps: LSD
Sugar Weed: Marijuana
Sunshine: LSD
Super X: Combination of methamphetamine and MDMA
Sweet Dreams: Heroin
Sweet Jesus: Heroin
Sweet Lucy: Marijuana
Sweet Stuff: Cocaine; heroin
Swell Up: Crack cocaine
Synthetic Cocaine: PCP

▶T
Tail Lights: LSD
Tab: LSD; cigarettes
Taste: Heroin; small sample of drugs
T-Buzz: PCP
Tea: Marijuana; PCP
Tea Party: Gathering where marijuana is smoked
Teardrops: Doses of crack packaged in cut-off corners of plastic bags
Tecatos: Hispanic heroin addict
Teenth: One-sixteenth of an ounce of cannabis
Texas Shoeshine: Inhalants
Thai Sticks: Bundles of marijuana soaked in hashish oil; marijuana
     buds bound to short sections of bamboo
THC: Tetrahydrocannabinol, the active ingredient in cannabis
Thinspiration: Advertisement or mass media event that promotes
     unhealthy weight loss or thinness

Thirty-eight: Crack cocaine sprinkled onto marijuana
Thrusters: Amphetamine
Tic: PCP in powder form; methamphetamine
Tigre (Spanish): Heroin
Tina: Methamphetamine; crystal methamphetamine; methamphetamine used with the erectile-dysfunction medication Viagra®
Tina: Crystal methamphetamine
Tits: Black-tar heroin
Toke: To snort cocaine; to smoke marijuana; marijuana
Toilet Water: Inhalants
Tolly: Toluene, a solvent
Top Gun: Crack cocaine
Tops: Peyote
Torch: Marijuana
Torch Cooking: Smoking cocaine freebase by using a propane lighter
Totally Spent: To have an MDMA hangover
Tranx: Tranquilizers
Trash: Methamphetamine
Tray: $3.00 bag of marijuana
Trey: Small rock of crack cocaine
Trip: High produced by LSD; high produced by MDMA
Tripping: High on drugs, especially LSD
Troll: To use LSD and MDMA
Troop: Crack cocaine
Turf: Place where drugs are sold
Turkey: Cocaine; amphetamine
Turnabout: Amphetamine
Tweaker: Methamphetamine user; also crack cocaine user who searches for drugs on the floor after a police raid
Tweak: Methamphetamine; to experience drug-induced paranoia; to peak on speed; to search desperately for crack cocaine
Tweak Mission: Search to find crack cocaine
Tweaks: Crack cocaine

Twin Towers: Heroin
Twist: Small plastic bag of heroin secured with a twist tie
Twistum: Marijuana cigarette
Tyler Berry: LSD combined with gasoline

▶U
Ultimate Xphoria: MDMA
Uppers: Stimulant drugs; amphetamine
Uppies: Amphetamine
Uptown: Cocaine
Uzi: Crack cocaine; crack pipe

▶V
Vega: Cigar wrapper refilled with marijuana
Vidrio: Heroin
Viper: Marijuana smoker
Viper's Weed: Marijuana
Vitamin A: The stimulant ADD medication Adderall®;
    amphetamines
Vitamin K: Ketamine
Vitamin R: Ritalin®
Vodka Acid: LSD

▶W
Wac: PCP sprinkled on marijuana
Wacky Weed: Marijuana
Waffle Dust: Combination of MDMA and amphetamine
Wake and Bake: Smoking marijuana in the morning
Wash: To prepare crack from cocaine powder; to recover drug
    residue from a spoon after injecting the drug
Water: Methamphetamine; PCP; mixture of marijuana and other
    substances within a cigar; GHB
Water Colors: LSD
Wedding Bells: LSD
Wedge: LSD

Weed: Cannabis in herbal form; marijuana; PCP
Weed Tea: Marijuana
Weight Trainers: Anabolic steroids
Whippets: Nitrous oxide
White Boy: Heroin; cocaine
White Ghost: Crack cocaine
White Girl: Cocaine; heroin
White Lightning: LSD
White Mosquito: Cocaine
White Powder: Cocaine; PCP
Whites: Amphetamine; folded papers used to wrap drugs
Whiz-Bang: Cocaine; combination of heroin and cocaine
Wicky: Combination of cocaine, PCP, and marijuana
Wicky Stick: PCP; combination of marijuana and crack cocaine
Wigging: Odd behavior resulting from the use of mind-altering drugs
Wildcat: Methcathinone (a stimulant similar to methamphetamine)
    mixed with cocaine
Window Glass: LSD
Wings: Cocaine; heroin
Winstrol V: Veterinary anabolic steroid
Witch: Cocaine; heroin
Wolf: PCP
Wolfies: Rohypnol®
Wollie: Rocks of crack cocaine rolled with marijuana into a cigar
Woolah Blunt: Marijuana and heroin combination
Woolah: Hollowed-out cigar refilled with marijuana and crack
    cocaine
Woolahs: Cigarettes laced with cocaine; crack cocaine sprinkled
    on a marijuana cigarette
Woolie: Combination of marijuana and heroin; combination of
    marijuana and crack cocaine
Wonder Star: Methcathinone (a stimulant similar to
    methamphetamine)
Work: Methamphetamine

Working Fifty: Crack cocaine rock weighing one-half gram or
    more
Wrap: Small folded paper packet used to hold powdered drugs,
    especially cocaine and speed
Wrecking Crew: Crack cocaine

▶ X

X: Ecstasy (MDMA); Marijuana; amphetamine
X-ing: Ecstasy (MDMA)
X-Pills: Ecstasy (MDMA)
XTC: Ecstasy (MDMA)

▶ Y

Yam: Crack cocaine
Yeah-O: Crack cocaine
Yellow Bullets: Depressants
Yellowjackets: Depressants; methamphetamine
Yerba Mala (Spanish): Marijuana
Yey: Cocaine
Yeyo (Spanish): Cocaine
Yolo: Cocaine

▶ Z

Z: One ounce of heroin
Zay: Mixture of marijuana and other drugs in a cigar
Zig-Zag Man: Marijuana; LSD; marijuana rolling paper
Zip: One ounce
Zombie: PCP; heavy user of drugs
Zoom: Marijuana laced with PCP; PCP
Zoomer: Person who sells fake crack cocaine and then flees
Zulu: Fake crack cocaine

Appendix B

READERS' RESOURCES

Al-Anon Family Group Headquarters
Al-Anon is a peer-led support group for the loved ones of addicted people. At meetings you can find encouragement, share strategies, and get concrete advice on how to help your teenager.

Phone: 757-563-1600
Toll free: 800-356-9996
Fax: 757-563-1655
Website: www.al-anon.alateen.org, www.al-anon.org
E-mail: afg@al-anon.org
Address:
1600 Corporate Landing Parkway
Virginia, VA 23454-5617

American Academy of Addiction Psychiatry (AAAP)
AAAP is the professional organization for psychiatrists and other clinicians who specialize in addiction. You can get referrals and information from its website.

Phone: 401-524-3076
Fax: 401-272-0922
Website: www.aaap.org
Email: information@aaap.org

Address:
345 Blackstone Blvd., Ste1, 1st Fl-Weld
Providence, RI 02906-4800

American Society of Addiction Medicine (ASAM)
ASAM is the professional organization for *physicians* who specialize
in addiction. You can get referrals and information from its website.

Phone: 301-656-3920
Fax: 301-656-3815
Website: www.asam.org
Email: email@asam.org
Address:
4601 N. Park Ave.
Upper Arcade, Ste 101
Chevy Chase, MD 20815-4519

Campaign for Tobacco-Free Kids
The organization provides information about teen smoking and
suggestions for keeping teenagers away from tobacco.

Phone: 202-296-5469
Fax: 202-296-5427
Website: www.tobaccofreekids.org
Email: info@tobaccofreekids.org
Address:
1400 I Street NW, Ste 1200
Washington, DC 20005-6531

Center on Addiction and the Family
COAF is a source of research data, support, and guidance for families struggling with addiction.

Phone: 1-888-671-9392
Website: www.phoenixhouse.org/family/center-on-addiction-and-
the-family

Address:
164 W. 74th St.
New York, NY 10023-2301

Narcotics Anonymous (NA)

A peer-led, 12-step-oriented support group, NA is best for those who use opioids or other illicit drugs, as opposed to alcohol alone. The national office can explain the group's general philosophy and provide meeting information.

Phone: 818-773-9999
Fax: 818-700-0700
Website: www.na.org
Email: info@na.org
Address:
19737 Nordhoff Place
Chatsworth, CA 91311-6606

National Association of Addiction Treatment Providers

An advocacy group for facilities that provide addiction treatment, the association maintains a website that can direct you to a wide variety of treatment facilities (mostly private).

Phone: 717-392-8480
Fax: 717-392-8481
Website: www.naatp.org
Email: rhunsicker@naatp.org
Address:
313 W. Liberty St.
Lancaster, PA 17603-2748

National Association on Drug Abuse Problems (NADAP)

This New York City–based program advises businesses about opening up employment opportunities for at-risk people. Its Substance Abuse Centralized Assessment Program prepares people with addiction for employment.

Phone: 212-986-1170
Fax: 212-697-2939
Website: www.nadap.org
Email: jdarin@nadap.org
Address:
355 Lexington Ave.
New York, NY 10017-6601

Substance Abuse and Mental Health Services Administration (SAMHSA) Publications Source
This is an excellent source of well-written, free educational materials about drugs, alcohol, and addiction.

Phone: 800-729-6686
Fax: 240-221-4292
Website: www.store.samhsa.gov
Address:
P.O. Box 2345
Rockville, MD 20847-2345

National Council on Alcoholism and Drug Dependence Inc. (NCADD)
NCADD provides advocacy information, resources for treatment, and self-assessment tools such as "Am I an Addict?" specially designed for teenagers. Ideal for a teen, or a parent, who might want to take an anonymous questionnaire about addiction.

Phone: 212-269-78797
Toll-free: 800-nca-call
Fax: 212-269-7510
Website: www.ncadd.org
Email: national@ncadd.org
Address:
22 Cortlandt St., Rm. 801
New York, NY 10007-3128

National Eating Disorders Association (NEDA)
The association provides information and referral suggestions for those with eating disorders. The public services announcements and personal stories available on the website describe the seriousness and potential lethality of eating disorders.

Phone: 206-382-3587
Toll-free: 800-931-2237
Fax: 206-829-8501
Website: www.nationaleatingdisorders.org
Email: info@nationaleatingdisorders.org
Address:
603 Stewart St., Ste 803
Seattle, WA 98101-1264

Physicians and Lawyers for National Drug Policy (PLNDP)
This research and advocacy organization focuses on sensible, data-based, legal and medical responses to addiction.

Phone: 401-863-6635
Fax: 401-444-1850
Web: www.plndp.org
Email: plndp@brown.edu
Address:
P.O. Box GBH
Providence, RI 02912-0001

Substance Abuse Referral Unit
This San Francisco-based organization arranges pretrial intervention for addicted people.

Phone: 415-626-5528
TTY: 415-626-4995
Fax: 415-626-3871
Website: www.sfpretrial.com

Email: will_leong@sfpretrial.com
Address:
567 7th St.
San Francisco, CA 94103-4709

Taylor Hooton Foundation
Educational site about the dangers of Anabolic Steroids

Phone: 972-403-7300
Website: www.taylorhooton.com
Address:
P. O. Box 2104
Frisco, TX 75034-9998

Treatment Communities of America
The organization provides information about the Therapeutic
Community (TC) philosophy, and practical suggestions about how
to gain admission to a TC.

Phone: 202-296-3503
Fax: 202-518-5475
Website: www.tcanet.org
Email: linda.tca@verizon.net
Address:
1601 Connecticut Ave., NW Ste 803
Washington, DC 20009-1055

Appendix C:

BIBLIOGRAPHY

Al-Anon Family Groups. www.al-anonfamilygroups.org/meetings/meeting.html.

Alateen Groups. www.al-anon.alateen.org/alateen.html.

Cancer Awareness. www.ecancerawareness.com.

Centers for Disease Control and Prevention. "Cigarette smoking-attributable morbidity—United States, 2000." *Morbidity and Mortality Weekly Report* 52 (2003): 842–844.

Consumer Nutrition and Health Information. www.fda.gov/food/labelingnutrition/consumerinformation/default.htm.

Daughton, J. M., and C. J. Kratochvil. "Review of ADHD Pharmacotherapies: Advantages, Disadvantages and Clinical Pearls." *Journal of the American Academy of Child & Adolescent Psychiatry* 48, no. 3 (March 2009): 240–248.

Devernsky, Jeffery L. and Rina Gupta. "Prevalence Estimates of Adolescent Gambling: A Comparison of SOGS-RA., DSM-IV-J and the GA 20 Questions." *Journal of Gambling Studies.* Vol. 16, Nos. 2–3 (2000): 227–252.

Johnston, Lloyd. "Trends in Harmfulness of Drugs as Perceived by 8th Graders," published online at Monitoring the Future. www.monitoringthefuture.org/data/09data.html#2009data-drugs90.

Johnston, Lloyd. "Trends in Lifetime Prevalence of Use of Various Drugs," published online at Monitoring the Future. www.monitoringthefuture.org/data/08data/pro8t1.pdf.

Lyon, Lindsey. "7 Reasons Parents Shouldn't Test Kids for Drug Use." *U.S. News and World Report*, August 6, 2008.

Mee-Lee, David et al. *ASAM Patient Placement Criteria for the Treatment of Substance-Related Disorders, Second Edition—Revised (ASAM PPC-2R)*. Chevy Chase, MD: American Society of Addiction Medicine, Inc., 2001.

Monitoring the Future. http://www.monitoringthefuture.org/data/10data/pr10t1.pdf.

Mentor Foundation. www.mentorfoundation.org/pdfs/prevention_perspectives/19.pdf.

Center for Disease Control. *Morbidity and Mortality Weekly Report,* Vol. 59, No. SS-5. June 4, 2010. www.cdc.gov/mmwr/pdf/ss/ss5905.pdf.

Rothman, Emily F. et al. "Relationship of Age of First Drink to Alcohol-Related Consequences among College Students with Unhealthy Alcohol Use." *Substance Abuse* 29 Number 1 (February 2008): 33–41.

"Salvia Trip," www.youtube.com/watch?v=RmPfj_4uqHQ.

Schaefer, Dick. *Choices & Consequences: What to Do When a Teenager Uses Alcohol/Drugs: A Step-by-Step System That Really Works*. Minneapolis: Johnson Institute Books, 1996.

Sexhelp.com, www.sexhelp.com.

State Department Fact Sheet on Behavior Modification Facilities. www.travel.state.gov/travel/tips/brochures/brochures_1220.html.

The American Academy of Pain Medicine, the American Pain Society, and the American Society of Addiction Medicine. *Definitions Related to the use of Opioids for the Treatment of Pain, A Consensus Document*. February, 2001.

The National Survey on Drug Use and Health (NSDUH), Office of Applied Studies, Substance Abuse and Mental Health Services Administration (SAMHSA). March 27, 2008.

The Ramones. "I Wanna Be Sedated." *Road to Ruin*. 1978, Sire Records.

"Trends in Lifetime Prevalence of Use of Various Drugs in Grades 8, 10, and 12." www.monitoringthefuture.org/data/o8data/pro8t1.pdf.

"Twenty Questions from Gamblers Anonymous." www.gamblersanonymous.org/20questions.html.

ACKNOWLEDGMENTS

I am deeply grateful to my teachers, among them Drs. Marc Galanter and Richard N. Rosenthal. Their personal examples of passion and dedication in the cause of helping the addicted person show a light for me and so many other clinicians. I have also learned from the parents and families of addicted teenagers, who told me what worked, and what did not, over the years. To those family members who anonymously reviewed drafts of this book and gave me their comments, I cannot thank you enough. Your courage and faith in facing your teenager's addiction has been truly inspiring to me. I am especially grateful to the following colleagues, who reviewed the manuscript and gave me priceless feedback: Andrew Evangelista, LCSW; Beth Berns, LCSW; and Eric Leventhal, LCSW.

Jonathan McCullough at Skyhorse Publishing made this a much better book with his insistence on clarity, relevance, and completeness in my message. Mel Parker, Constance Johnson, Christina Pumariega, and Amanda McElroy gave me invaluable assistance in making my message coherent, and my attorney, Eric Brown, kept me focused on what I was trying to do. Ann Dunn and Christine Schubert worked tirelessly verifying sources, collating documents, and making the manuscript presentable.

Finally, I deeply appreciate the love and support of Lisa, Noah, Tali, and Ari, all of whom went above and beyond the call of duty in countenancing my writing binges, and even kept me company in our "Study Parties." I could not have done it without you!

INDEX